Comin' In Over the Rock: A Storyteller's History of Cannon Beach

REVISED EDITION

By Peter Lindsey

2016

Comin' In Over the Rock: A Storyteller's History of Cannon Beach
Revised Edition
© 2016 **Peter Lindsey**
ISBN13: 978-1-932010-87-9

Cover design by **Peter Grant**
Back cover photograph by **Kim Logan**
Interior design by **Bess Pallares**

Printed in the United States of America

I would like to dedicate this edition of my book to Jyanai Morse and Jack Brown, who, through their example, have shown me the way.

My idea of a good society is Cannon Beach in the 1940s when I came here. There was very little money circulating, things were inexpensive, it wasn't crowded, we had no police, no city, and no crime. First we got the city, then we got the police, then we got crime.

—*Frank Hammond*

Contents

Editor's Note

Comin' In Over the Rock was originally published in 2004. Now, over a decade later, a number of people and places from the original edition no longer exist. We could have updated the material but felt that it would disrupt the flow of Peter's stories and create an unnecessary level of editorial footnotes, so we left the narratives as they were written. To compensate, we added new stories to the collection.

Acknowledgments

Many hands and minds labored long and hard to bring the revised edition of my book to fruition. I am particularly indebted to the following people for their yeomen's service on my behalf. Rainmar Bartl, Tracy Abel, Rex and Diane Amos, Lorraine Mercer, Robert Mercer, Per Henningsgaard, Abbey Gaterud, Chelsea Lobey, Kellie Doherty, Deborah Mersereau, and Maureen Dooley-Sroufe devoted copious hours of their precious time to the project. Karl Marlantes and Sally Lackaff created introductions and, in Sally's case, a new map for this edition. Peter Grant crafted a stellar new cover for the revised edition and collated historical photographs and graphic materials.

Legions of individuals provided anecdotes and reminiscences for the creation of this text's body and soul. I would particularly like to thank the Sroufe family, John Rippey, Prissy Martin, Betsy Ayres, Karolyn Adamson, Leonard Gerritse, Les Ordway, Frank and Roland Picard, Frank Lackaff, and George Shields. Tyler Evans resurrected the original manuscript from the bowels of my computer, for which I'm most grateful.

In pursuing the revised edition of *Comin' In Over the Rock*, my paltry fiscal straits posed a significant obstacle. My mentors suggested a benefit. I was dubious, but they prevailed. The response was gratifying in the extreme. As a consequence of a tsunami wave of generous gifts, this book will hit the bookshelves in the near future. To all those who donated on my behalf, I extend heartfelt thanks. Among those who donated substantial funds were the following: Mike, Stacy, and Will Benefield; Rex and Diane Amos; Ron Logan; Jim, Jody, Max, and Luke Babson; Tommy Misner and Peggy Roberti; Bill Hayes and Diane Jackson; Bud Clark; Scott Rekate;

Carol Newman; Gary and Marlene Laws; Daniel and Michele Floyd; Tim Keller; Betsy Ayres; Leslie Ryan (in memory of Valerie Ryan); Cleveland and Marilyn Rooper; Charlene Larsen; Tom and Kate Merrell; Mike Morgan; Lorraine Ortiz; Scott Ecketein and Karin Hermansen; Susan Ogilvie; Barb and Mike Knop; Julie Walker; Charlotte Rubin; Jean Williams; Robin Risley and Tommy Huntington; Dale and Linda Hintz; Laurie Beers; Tracy Abel and Todd Riley; Jason Houck; Dave Simmons; Pax Broder; Clayton Rippey and Libby Hedden; Jo Rudnic Olson; Maryann and Steven Sinkler; John Rippey; Barry Marshall and Barb Rippey; Gerald Sroufe and Maureen Dooley-Sroufe; John and Deborah Mersereau; Bill and Tammy Ellis; Jay and Elizabeth Raskin; Duane and Cheryl Johnson; and Joe Hummel.

Peter Lindsey, December 2015

Foreword to the First Edition

As someone who started life several times in Cannon Beach, I value Peter's book as a sacred and sweet thing, encapsulating the place and community I have loved all my life. This work of Peter's evokes for me a taste of the Cannon Beach I felt as a child living in midtown, where streets had no need to be paved and the beach and friendly forest were always predominant neighbors. It is such a treat to sense through another's pen the same warmth, kinship, comfort, and character that always seemed an inherent atmosphere. I love Peter's humorous touches and his shaping of story into a familiar voice. Having indeed been familiar with Peter for most of my life, this closeness grows when reading of his youthful exploits and regional excursions in company with some of my own loved kith and kin, seen from angles I was born too late to be privy to. These stories I treasure the most.

Through his rosy lens, the history and sensibility of Cannon Beach take on a distinctive life. The people shaping the story have faces and voices; the aroma of salt air seems to emanate from his descriptions. I welcome this book as an unquestionable resource for myself and all those who hold on to the tentative and tender romance of this place we love.

Sally Lackaff

Foreword to the Revised Edition

Histories inform; stories connect. These stories connect the reader with a time when you could feel the ground vibrating as a log truck rumbled right through the center of town loaded to its weight limit, or maybe just a little bit over, with just one huge old-growth log. Today the log trucks travel on bypass highways, whizzing past Taco Bells and Pizza Huts, carrying twenty-five or more slender logs that back in the day were called pecker poles.

Back then, logging wasn't romantic; it was a job. It was a fascinating and exhilarating one, no doubt, because it was dangerous. It still is. Five of my friends lost their fathers to logging accidents before I was out of high school.

Loggers and their families could afford to live in Cannon Beach back then. Today that logger's home is the second home of a professional couple from Portland with a Mercedes station wagon parked in front and occupied maybe a quarter of the time. I have to confess, my wife and I own one of those old logger's houses too, only we live up by Seattle and drive a Volvo.

I, however, am a native. I grew up here. I might have left town, but my heart stayed.

Peter and I were in high school together. The friend helping Peter run the clandestine radio station in one of Peter's stories was my cousin, Gary. Reading Peter's stories, I am pulled back to the "old days" and they will pull you back, too, even if you didn't live them as Peter and I did.

Just after reading Peter's book, I walked past the Coaster Theater, which I usually do quite unconsciously. This time, memories of the old skating rink and dancehall that used to stand there flooded me. Because of reading Peter's stories, I was reconnected with the time, the music, and the *feeling* of cool summer nights, the possibility of meeting a beautiful girl, of Paul Revere and the Raiders out of Boise, Idaho, or the Wailers out of Tacoma, Washington, or any number of earnest rock groups making a buck playing until midnight, hoping some day they would go national.

This time, as I continued down Hemlock Street, I was once again connected with the feel of the old wooden sidewalk, splintered by loggers' caulk boots, under my feet. Instead of the vacation condos at the north end of Hemlock, I was reconnected with the old service station where kids would hang out in the warm office as the rain slashed down on the dirty windows, the smell of oil in the air, the candy bars for sale, their wrappers dirty with the oil from the hand of someone who thought they might buy, but didn't.

There was more innocence back then, and I miss that. One could also call it naivety, however. The local papers didn't report murders in Baltimore and missing children didn't stare at you from your milk carton at breakfast. Still, we all knew who couldn't go home after work without first stopping for a beer at Bill's Tavern and then staying until closing time—at least if it was pay day. We all knew who was messing around and with whom. We also knew who needed help, even if they'd never ask for it—and we helped—and we gossiped.

Reading Peter's stories, I am made conscious of how things change and have changed. There were no surfers then. They started showing up in the late fifties with long heavy boards and no wet suits. They weren't tougher, just colder. We only had big crowds on the Fourth of July and Labor Day, but now there are crowds on any nice weekend. To get to Portland, we drove the "Wolf Creek Highway," in parts still gravel, and it took several hours, but that included a required stop at Oney's Tavern and Restaurant in Elsie, or Staley's Café at the Vernonia junction. It is now Highway 26, takes ninety minutes, and Oney's and Staley's are gone. There was a rock road that led from Highway 101 down through the spruce trees to the beach where Haystack Rock stands. Today that road connects to driveways of vacation homes.

Attitudes and ways of thinking have changed as well as the physical landscape. We didn't have tsunami evacuation routes. We expected people to use common sense and get to high ground. It sounds like I'm bragging about that attitude; I suppose I am. I think people were tougher and tougher-minded back then. On the other hand, it was my generation who put in the tsunami warning system, and I wouldn't want it otherwise. It's just that we never thought about the trade-offs, the death by a thousand cuts. Yes, we're safer today, but an odd, unintended consequence is that we're more frightened and we forget that for each added safety measure there is a cost—in beauty, in freedom, and in engagement with the natural world. We brilliantly light the beach and our streets at night, but we no longer see the stars.

There's no putting the clock back, but with Peter's stories, you have the next best thing. If we did have time machines, most of us wouldn't have a clue what to look for; but by reading these stories, you experience a world shaped by a sensitive soul, with routes and landmarks selected and highlighted for your journey.

Karl Marlantes

Haystack Rock from Ecola Ramp (Grant/Bartl Collection)

Introduction

"She's comin' in over the rock today, boys!" George would comment as the rain slashed at the windows of the shambling, yellow-washed building. Five or six of us were slouched and huddled around the old oil stove at Malstead's Shell Station in Cannon Beach. The station sat on the corner of Gower Street and Hemlock, north of Haystack Rock, although there was no Gower Street then. The year was 1957. Several of us were hormone-addled teenagers, filled with visions of souped-up Chevrolets and nights at the drive-in movies. We called George Malstead "Happy Tooth" because he perpetually grinned, tolerated us in the recesses of his rattly old weathered garage, and generally filled the gaps in young adolescent boys' lives with stories and a constant string of fascinating patrons. When the dogs of winter howled and snapped at the single-walled, shingled old service station, George would hole up with us in the office. What I would describe, to be gentle, as "characters" spirited in and out of the building; stopped to comment on the nature of existence; regaled us with stories of logging, fishing, women, fighting, and the old days; and generally enchanted the imagination of a sixteen-year-old boy.

The stories and the characters stuck in a way that affected me deeply. What would we be without stories? I feel privileged to have known those times and people, many of whom made this village of Cannon Beach what it has become in the collective imagination. For many years I have hoped to devote some days to sharing those anecdotes and memories of a place and times passed. Perhaps I am singularly equipped to do so at this late date. We Lindseys have been rich in stories. My father, Harvey Lindsey, was an extraordinary raconteur. He sat on the first city council in Cannon Beach, a body that formulated the first set of laws and regulations for the city. Included were laws prohibiting swearing and urinating outdoors within the city limits and a plan for lighting the beachfront to avoid "spooning" on the beach. He resigned after two meetings, chagrined that he had violated two of the ordinances on his way home from the city office. This story will be an account of the village I have known, some of its history, and its characters. If I err on the side of historical veracity, so be it. I hope the account will serve to flesh out in some small way those people and the place they occupied in an earlier day.

As I sit at my desk this February day, the rain-filled southwest winds buffet the second-growth hemlock and spruce outside, snarling and snuffling through the trunks and branches, gnawing, eroding, yet nurturing the land I have known and loved. This is a north coast day. The weather is, indeed, coming in over Haystack Rock. It's winter. The long, dark time. A time of stories. I salute the many souls who have lived and died in this place and made it a place so many cherish. To the Gerritses, Paul Bartels, Tommy Stanton, Gainor Minott, Mac and Mae McCoy, the Ordways, George Malstead and the rest, this is your story as I know it and had it told to me. I pray I can do it justice. Please excuse my inadequacies, deficiencies, and failure of memory. The inexorable spread of "progress" over the landscape has rapidly transformed the terrain and the township it occupies. Just a few generations ago, Cannon Beach was a settlement of barely fifty souls, very rural, darkly wooded. Perhaps I can exhume a few circumstances and personalities to help you see those days more clearly. I'll begin with my beginnings here.

My first introduction to Cannon Beach was in the summer of 1946. The Lindseys had rented Nate Cozey's cottage on First Street, just west of the Waves Roller Rink. The permanent residences and cottages had blackout curtains to mask the interior lighting from Japanese aircraft during

Kraemer Point (Tom Olsen Collection)

nighttime hours. Families summered here. The same scant number of families returned year after year, regular as the seasons. It was a village of boardwalks, a few mercantile stores, a skating rink, post office, bakery, shingled cottages, a handful of permanent residences, a church, a riding stable, a gas station or two, and a couple of restaurants. The plethora of trinket and souvenir shops we take for granted characterized Seaside, not Cannon Beach. My family established a recreational beachhead below Kraemer Point, the current location of the nuns' retreat, and lived on the beach during the daylight hours. Both my mother and father had spent considerable periods of time at Cannon Beach and the north coast. My father surveyed the area around Chinook, Washington, in 1908, and the Lindseys owned a family home on S. Columbia in Seaside at the turn of the century. My mother spent her youth in Cannon Beach, swimming in the surf and riding horses at Spaulding's Riding Academy on Elk Creek.

We moved to Cannon Beach in the early 1950s. My father built the house we occupied in 1956 virtually single-handedly. Paul Bartels, an early homesteader, helped him build the chimney. Ed Klever, another old-timer, shingled the roof. In my youth and early manhood, I was free to range the beaches and headlands, fish the streams, and hunt in the timbered foothills.

As the years passed, I became increasingly interested in the history of this place. Who were the early people? How did they arrive here? How did they work and pass the time? Where were the actual sites of early homesteads? What stories did these sojourners have to tell? What was unique about the place? Who were the quirky and singular characters?

I guess I began, almost unconsciously, to develop some sense of the place by listening to the land itself. Over the years, I've rambled, slogged, coursed through every square foot of terrain within a day's tromp of Cannon Beach. I've gotten to know the headlands and forested promontories, the creeks, rivers, rivulets, beaches, coves, trails, and mountains better than most. In the company of my old friend Bob Gilmore, I've probed the earth under home sites and old settlements. The earth itself talks to you if you listen. The maps of history, or at least the traces and hints, are underfoot, if you sharpen vision.

I can tell you where the early indigenous people, the Clatsops, feasted and camped. Bob and I probed old middens, massive shell garbage dumps common to people of the northwest coast. Indian Beach, mentioned by Lewis and Clark as a site of Indian encampment, has a fine midden. Graded over by Caterpillars excavating for a military road to the top of Tillamook Head in the 1940s, this location has provided mammal bones, fire-cracked rock, shell fragments, teeth, and other detritus. Other sites exist at the early Frank Brallier homestead on Brallier Road, on Ecola Point, and south of Silver Point (formerly Sylvan Point). An Indian settlement of some consequence was situated at the present location of the Cannon Beach School. William Clark's journal refers to this place as "a Village of 5 Cabins . . . on Ecola or Whale Creek." Public works projects have occasionally unearthed artifacts at this location.[1]

Bob Gilmore (Grant/Barl Collection)

---

[1] *At various times in Cannon Beach's history, Lewis and Clark's Ecola Creek has been called Ecola Creek and Elk Creek.*

Logging camp (Lent Collection)

If the asphalt and buildings were removed there and the earth combed by archaeologists, I suspect many interesting items could be located even today. When one visits these places, it is easy to see why early people opted for them as choice natural prospects. Streams debouch into the ocean, making plentiful freshwater available. Migrating fish stocks use the streambeds for travel. Shellfish abound on shoreside rock outcrops. Pleasingly level ground and aesthetic vistas distinguish each of them. You and I would choose these places, intuitively, today.

Pioneers to our area, taking a page from Johnny Appleseed, quickly established small orchards near their cabins. Fruit trees, especially when blooming in springtime, suggested sites of old homesteads, some harking back to the late 1800s. The trees, predominantly apples, stand out to the observer's eye against a backdrop of conifers: the native hemlock and Sitka spruce. Armed with long metal probes and shovels, Gilmore and I groveled in the forest duff like truffle pigs for artifacts. Together we worked through the forest floor in the bottomland on the old pipeline trail near Elk Creek. Antique bottles, old woodstove finials, and china plates were our treasure. We also mined the old Anderson homestead. An old holly tree gave us the clue here.

Half a mile southwest of the Cannon Beach Junction, we located a particularly rich site. Subsequent research has informed me that a logging camp situated there housed early spruce loggers just after the century's turn. Bob and I didn't know that then. We simply followed the clues. On a fine spring day several decades ago, we slashed through bracken and skunk cabbage to an elevated roadbed. A small railroad trunk line had traversed this woodland and terminated at a logging camp. Trunk lines from this camp, Les Ordway informed me, snaked up near Circle Creek and in along the Radar Road path almost to Indian Beach. The loggers extracted huge spruce from sites along the track behind Tillamook Head. Substantial lumps of coal had hinted at early habitation. Digging through the rich humus we unearthed rusted gears, rugged English china plates, apothecary vials, stove parts, and hand-blown gin and whiskey bottles.

Over the years, in company with Gilmore and Frank Lackaff, I've located many places chosen by our predecessors as homestead sites. One of them sat just south of the Arch Cape Shingle Mill on Arch Cape Creek. Located on the trail that crossed Arch Cape, this small cabin and its occupants served travelers heading south over Neahkahnie Mountain. In an earlier day, fruit trees and a small vegetable garden provided passersby with some small provisions for the journey down the coast. On a side hill amongst fern, tangled root wads, and windfall, we located quite a number of jettisoned bottles and materiel. Garbage wasn't collected in those days. Folks just chucked it out the back door into a convenient ravine and called it good. Other locations we investigated were behind Hug Point, at the old Gerritse mill at the foot of Ecola Park Road, and near a crabapple grove in the Elk Creek bottomland east of the Elk Creek Bridge. This was the old Stoddard place. Bob Gilmore stayed in a cabin on the original property in the early 1970s.

Even in the present day, excavators digging foundations unearth shards and reminders of those early times: an old horseshoe, kerosene lantern parts, an encrusted chisel. Parts of John and Mary Gerritse's wagon, crumpled and wrecked in an early accident, lay moldering and rusting in a ditch on Gerritse Creek when I was a boy: singletree, rusted wheels, decayed wood. If one nosed around there today, I imagine traces could still be located.

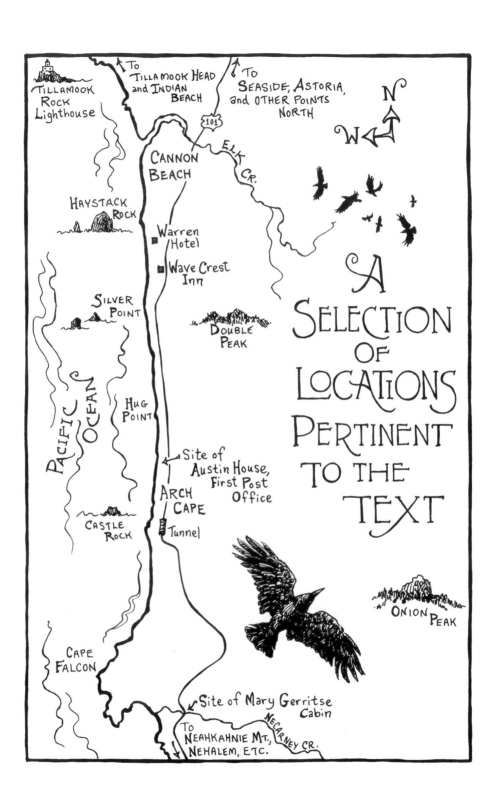

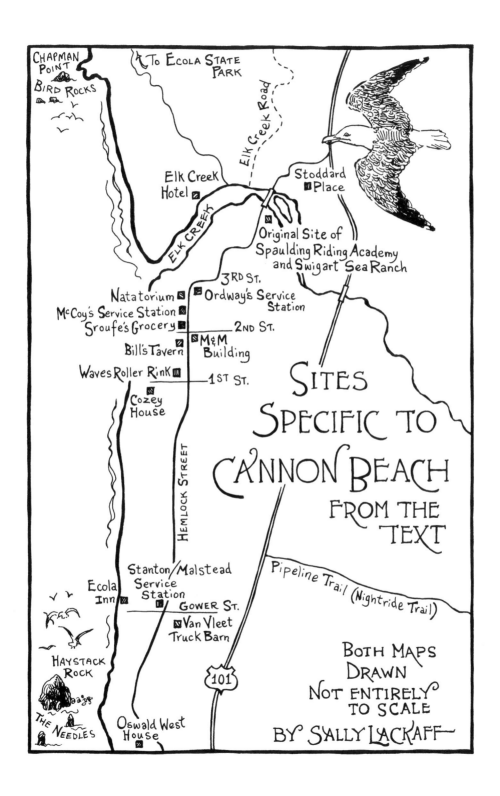

Chapter 1
Early Arrivals

Mary Gerritse's Journal

How did the earliest travelers and settlers get to this piece of coastline? What salient natural features and prospects greeted them on arrival? By the mid-1800s, barring shipwreck or other travail, most (and they were scant numbers indeed) took one of two routes to what is now Cannon Beach. The following excerpt from Mary Gerritse's journal describes how her family travelled from the Willamette Valley to Nehalem. From Nehalem one crossed Neahkahnie Mountain and the capes and headlands over primitive Indian trails, eventually arriving at present-day Cannon Beach.

Mary Gerritse, later in life (Clatsop County Historical Society)

"We travelled by team over the mountains on the North Yamhill Road, which is not used now. It was a mail route at that time. Sometimes the mail carrier had to cross over it on snowshoes. It took a week or ten days to go from Scholls Ferry to Tillamook. We spent a night at Tillamook, then called Hoquarton, and took a boat from there to Garibaldi. There were no hotels or inns.... the settlers all welcomed travellers and helped them along. We got another team to carry our things from Garibaldi to the Nehalem River, then took them by boat up the river."

Early Routes to Cannon Beach

The second route began with a downriver boat ride from the Willamette Valley to Astoria. Parties crossed Youngs Bay to Skipanon Landing and Lexington at the mouth of the Lewis and Clark River. By boat or canoe (and probably some portage) one reached Clatsop Plains. Seasonally dismal marsh and rolling foredune carried toward Tillamook Head at the south of the plains. At that point matters became very dicey indeed. Three trails crossed Tillamook Head. The easternmost trail was later improved as a wagon road constructed of puncheon or corduroy, logs laid in mud, by the late 1800s. In its earliest configuration, though, it was simply a trail through thicket and briar.

Travelled by J. H. Frost of the Wilkes Expedition in 1841, the route was described thus: "The briers and bushes were ten or twelve feet high, and very thickly interwoven." This track followed, roughly, the current-day road from Seaside to Cannon Beach. The westernmost route was an Indian trail, the same used by Lewis and Clark in 1805 to reach a whale stranded at Ecola Creek mouth. Leaving the cove north of Tillamook Head, one hiked along the beach over boulders heading south, until reaching an impassable rock outcrop on the beach. At that point one scaled steep cliffs to the top of the head, dropped down to Indian Beach, climbed over two headlands, and walked south to Elk Creek. An additional route crossed the headland east of Canyon Creek and took one eventually to Elk Creek. Both Tillamook Head and Neahkahnie were nemeses of bypass, but the latter was most treacherous.

J. H. Frost described the trail over Neahkahnie as "the width of a man's two hands, stony and gravelly." Asked by a prospective adventurer which parts were the most difficult, he said they were "all the most difficult." Some of the earliest crossers, members of the Wilkes Expedition, walked on hands and knees on this trail.

The Natural Environs of Cannon Beach

The first pioneer arrivals encountered a densely wooded littoral region. The capes and heads and the foothills behind them thrust massive stands of ancient Sitka spruce skyward. A shadowed walk beneath their magnitude can only be imagined in this age of industrial forestry. To occupy

Sitka spruce along Elk Creek Road (Tom Olsen Collection)

and secure a 160-acre homestead, one had to prove up, as settlers phrased it, a parcel of land. Clearing stands of timber and disposing of bucked logs and branches characterized most early years of homesteading in the Northwest. Early photos indicate dense stands of timber right up to the shoreline barely penetrable by sunlight. Homesteaders bored holes in stumps with a two-inch auger, one horizontally into a trunk and one above it diagonally connecting with the first. Burning embers inserted into holes and teased with a bellows eventually scorched away stumpage and huge logs. Many early cabins at what was then called Ecola relied on split-cedar planking and framework for walls and long cedar shakes for roofs.

Chapter 2
Founding Families and Early Odd Ducks

I think it would be pertinent at this time to consider some of the first people to live in Cannon Beach, the founding families—and some solitary souls—who gave this emerging township what we now consider its "village character," its unique shape and spirit. By all counts Mary Gerritse evinces that peculiar individuality, that spunk, that tendency to fly in the face of contemporary convention that we town folk seem to relish even today. Mary was diminutive in stature (she never weighed more than one hundred pounds in her life), yet she loomed large in the chronicles of her time. In the 1880s her family homesteaded in Manzanita at the foot of Neahkahnie Mountain.

One day, Mary, in her teens, was rounding up the family's cows on the slope of Neahkahnie near the perilous trail over the mountain. I think this anecdote suggests, in subtle ways, what Mark Twain would have termed "the sand" that characterized this woman. From her own words:

*William Warren's first cabin
(Stevens Collection)*

> *One day while up on the mountain pasture rounding up the cows, I met three young men coming from Seaside to Nehalem over the old mail trail. They*

Neahkahnie Trail (Lent Collection)

were surprised to see a girl in that wilderness. One of them was a young Dutch sailor named John Gerritse who had decided he wanted to remain in America and had deserted his ship in Astoria. The other two were Nehalem boys. John asked them who the girl was and asked if that was the best that Nehalem had. Albert said, "Well, that's one of them." John said, "I don't think much of them then." The boys passed on and it was several years before John [her future husband] and I met at a party.

Following marriage and the birth of a child, John and Mary filed a "squatter's claim" on a preemptive homestead. A squatter's claim could only be made on unsurveyed land, for forty acres, on which a cabin had to be built. Squatters had to stay on the land. They built a cabin on the side of Necarney Creek, just under the south end of the modern-day bridge south of Oswald West State Park. The small cabin was built from materials gleaned from the land. Split cedar boards nine feet long for walls and three-foot cedar shakes for the roof. Hewn driftwood planks scavenged from the beach below constituted flooring.

From the 1890s until the early 1900s, John and Mary Gerritse, J. E. Brallier from Seaside, and Phil Condit carried the mail on two routes

Mail carrier at Hug Point (Tom Olsen Collection)

from Seaside to Nehalem Valley and Tillamook; no mean feat, assuredly. The Gerritses later also hauled freight and passengers over the primitive road from Seaside to Elk Creek by wagon and buckboard. Riders used the beach itself whenever the surf made headlands passable. Hug Point was the bane of early travelers and continued to pose threats to horse and auto as late as the 1960s, as we shall see. J. E. Brallier nearly drowned in a crab hole offshore when his foot caught in a stirrup. Mary's beloved horse Prince perished in strong surf at its base.

What might be termed the "ocean mail route" left the Austin House (Austin House was originally designated the official location of the Cannon Beach Post Office) south of Hug Point. Riding south on the beach to Arch Cape, carriers then either skirted Arch Cape at low tide or took an inland route over the cape, behind Cape Falcon and over the precipitous trail on Neahkahnie and on into the Nehalem Valley and the Onion Peak Post Office, located on the Scovell ranch at Hobsonville. An inland mail route left south Seaside over trail and corduroy road (roughly following the Highway 26 route of our time) and stopped at the Herman Ahlers farm, called the Push Post Office, about ten miles southeast of Seaside. (The Hamlet Grange and the fire hall currently stand at this location.) The carrier turned south at Black Bridge and headed for Buchanan Creek, then passed northeast of Onion Peak and on to the North Fork of the Nehalem River and the Onion Peak Post Office (Les Ordway called this the Buchanan Trail—some accounts call this the Onion Peak Trail). Another trail in the area, somewhat later, led to the top of Sugarloaf Mountain where a fire lookout stood. Mary

Austin House, first Cannon Beach Post Office, late 1800s (Clatsop County Historical Society)

confessed to enjoying this ride; on fine days she paused long enough to catch a few fish for the evening meal on the river.

In her days as homesteader and carrier, she persevered in the face of rigors inconceivable to most of us. She gave birth to a child in a lonely squatter's shack seven miles from the nearest human habitation by trail, had horses swept from under her by fierce surf, tumbled astride her faithful horse Prince down the scarps of Neahkahnie, found herself completely burned out by fire and homeless in Nehalem, menaced by bears and cougars, daunted by downed trees and quagmire, and chided by proper neighbors:

"When I carried the mail, I rode astride on a saddle. I got a lot of criticism because it was not ladylike. I wore boots and overalls, had a thin skirt to button on over the overalls to keep from shocking the neighbors. What was the difference? I was not doing a lady's work anyway!"

I would nominate Mary Gerritse as candidate for First Lady of Cannon Beach. Her like are rarely encountered in any time or place.

I would like to catalog significant families and loners who shared time and place with the Gerritses. The Bralliers, Mansurs, Austins, Carnahans, Sabines, Claytons, Andersons, Warrens, Bartels, Logans, and Adairs settled and lived their stories. A handful of loners, mostly bachelors and some remittance men, established a tradition that exists in Cannon Beach, I would suggest, to this day. Remittance men, not unlike some trust funders today, gravitated to the coast to live their solitary lives: odd ducks, misfits, black sheep, miscreants, square pegs, dissolutes, dreamers, recluses. Some received financial assistance, genteel "stay away" subsistence money. Others merely sought to avoid the pratfalls of marriage and responsibility.

Numbered among these colorful bachelor characters, some earlier and many later, are such notables as James Mehan recalled by most as "Jimmie the Tough," Joe Walsh, Bill Kruschke—"the Hermit of Falcon Cove," Indian Louis, "Smitty" Smith, and Jim Ellis. James Mehan had jumped ship in Astoria. Of English or Irish descent, Mehan, by most accounts, holed up in a makeshift cabin just north of Silver Point, liked spirits, stayed through the tides on Jockey Cap fishing and sold his catch locally, scuffled periodically, and, like Walsh, traipsed over the trail to Seaside, when the coffers allowed, to catch a snoot full. Joe Walsh settled on a good land claim just north of Arch Cape. Gaming and drink lured him to Seaside, often mounted on an old horse. Walsh periodically careened along the beach with wobbly boots. Several oral history informants describe his arrival on the beach, pixilated, stumbling off his horse into piles of driftwood, completely befuddled.

Indian Louis lived on Mail Creek out Necanicum way but ranged around Ecola and Cannon Beach. Early pioneers speak warmly of this trapper and hunter who shared his cabin and provender. In his rough-hewn shake cabin, Louis smoked slabs of meat in a mud fireplace. His geniality and graciousness won great favor. Those passing his cabin stopped to palaver, water and feed horses, accept his hospitality. Louis delivered smoke-cured game to homesteaders in Seaside and Cannon Beach. Some pioneers referred to him as "Banjo Louie" because he played a homemade banjo fashioned from a five-gallon coal oil can. He's also remembered for aiding J. E. Brallier, a mail rider, when Brallier foundered in the surf at Hug Point.

Turn of the Century Settlers

At the turn of the century Ecola (later called Cannon Beach) and the environs south still existed as locales somewhat off the track. If you placed yourself in a crow's eye and flew north along the beach just after the

Elk Creek Hotel (Clatsop County Historical Society)

turn of the century, these are some of the significant structures in your ken. The Arch Cape Hotel was situated oceanfront, near the present Maxwell Avenue. Nearby sat Marmaduke Maxwell's cabin. Marmaduke, a character very warmly regarded by his Arch Cape neighbors, kept a small herd of cows that grazed near his cabin. Pictures in the recent *Arch Cape Chronicles* show Marmaduke taking his little jitney buggy down the beach toward Cannon Beach. A white-maned, whiskery gentleman, he had a jaunty, sturdy look about him. Other photographs depict Maxwell's cattle drives down the strip of shoreline. Farther north Joe Walsh's homestead and barn reposed. The Austin House (Cannon Beach's first official post office) lay south of Hug Point. The Mansur/ Settum dwellings shelved up above the beach south of Silver Point. Frank Brallier's dairy and homestead occupied the beachfront north of Silver Point. The Warren brothers' homesteads lay in low level ground roughly midway between Haystack Rock and Silver Point. Some habitation sat on Kraemer Point. The Sutherland House perched on the foredune above the mouth of Elk Creek, and a lifesaving station occupied the tip of Ecola Point. Logan's Elk Creek Hotel, first called the Logan

William Warren's second cabin (Stevens Collection)

House, rested just north of the creek at the terminus of the wagon road from Seaside.

A wagon trip to Cannon Beach from Seaside sounds like the Bataan Death March. The road, a quagmire in winter, followed old trail courses. A four-horse stage or buckboard forded the Necanicum River, stopped at what was called Halfway House to water horses, then continued across the flank of Tillamook Head to the north bank of Elk Creek. At low tide, the wagon crossed the creek and pointed south down the beach. Lodging at Elk Creek Hotel was available. If two wagons met on the road at one time, one wagon generally dismantled teams and let the other pass. Drivers bellowed in narrow defiles to see if the narrow road was clear. Passengers fording Elk Creek suffered discouraging wettings in swollen stream conditions.

Before the Lanpheres and Mr. Sheets established their first stores in Cannon Beach, supplies had to be trucked in by the same tortuously curved wagon road. Joe Walsh and Frank Brallier raised small herds of dairy cows for product. Walsh also ran a few head of cattle. Fresh milk, cream, and butter supplemented diets from the earliest days. Many families put up salt pork, raised or stowed away apples, potatoes, vegetables, cabbages, and onions. Salmon could be purchased for twenty-five cents. A smorgasbord of bounteous game and shellfish filled in the gaps nicely. We'll hint at the plenitude later.

Frank Brallier

I would like to consider Frank Ellis Brallier, his background and wan-

Elk Creek-Cannon Beach Stage (Cannon Beach Conference Center Collection)

derings, in some detail. He seems to me to typify the character of many of the most memorable pioneers. A strong and unique personality, the existence he chiseled out for himself and his family exemplifies what we cherish in the image of our forefathers. Like most who found themselves here, his antecedents were European. Escaping the Alsace region along the Rhine, his forbears sailed to Jamaica, ran afoul of yellow fever, worked as indentured laborers in Philadelphia, sweated and toiled, flowed west with dreams of gold and land ownership, settled in McMinnville and then Warrenton at the end of the nineteenth century. In the vast tracts of land, the apparently limitless raw resources and timber stands unequalled anywhere in the world, Frank recognized an untrammeled jewel of coastline and sea. It lured one in ways exceeding even the spell of gold.

In this place on the Oregon coast, Frank Brallier would carve a spot for himself, his family, and his heirs. He was born in Tillamook in 1866. In the Oregon territory of 1890, our piece of coastline had no roads. Like the Mansurs who arrived at about the same time, the Bralliers were a tough breed. As his grandson put it, "When they came, they came to stay!" Their first homestead building, a rough-hewn cedar shack, had a mud fireplace and few amenities. The first white child born in Cannon Beach, Louretta, was born in this crude building in 1907. When the child's birth seemed imminent, a midwife was summoned to aid in the delivery. The tide that day proved so high that the midwife couldn't reach the Brallier homestead. Frank delivered the child himself.

Frank improved the land and installed a barn and outbuildings. He developed a waterworks. Mail delivery came via Mary or John Gerritse, who retrieved letters and parcels from a leather bag hung from a post on the beach. Frank and his brothers, Jake and John, established timber claims beyond the site in the hills. He designated the area Wave Crest. In the 1890s his diminutive dairy farm provided a livelihood for his family and products for the settlers.

His shoreside location and scant tillable land made pasturage extremely problematic. Undaunted, Brallier drove his dairy cows each morning south along the beach and around Sylvan Point to a postage stamp of grassland just north of the Mansur claim above the sea. An early settler, Mrs. Randall, described her visual recollection of the Bralliers taking the cows to pasture each morning:

One of the happy memories of early Cannon Beach was that of Mrs. Brallier in the early morning in her cotton-blue dress, right against the sea, taking the Jersey cows to Sylvan Point. Mr. Brallier was equally picturesque, a very slender person wearing a short brown waterproof cape made of three layers that reached to his waist. They could have been painted or sketched effectively. They made a lovely pastoral scene.

Despite the rich resources, subsistence was difficult for many. The Bralliers shared their means with less fortunate neighbors. As Don Osborne, Frank Brallier's grandson suggests, families like the Bartels, scratching by in those hard times, relied on what the land provided. Odd jobs, hunting, wood cutting, and fishing supported them in meager fashion. The Bralliers often took meals to people like the Bartels to tide them over in lean times. Six generations of Bralliers and their progeny have occupied the land in south Tolovana Park until this day.

Events at the Turn of the Century

A number of significant historical events transpired in the 1880s and early 1900s. The Tillamook Lighthouse construction began in 1880 and continued through the following year. A major engineering feat, its value as a sentinel for mariners became painfully apparent. During its construction,

Tillamook Rock Lighthouse (Lent Collection)

the bark *Lupatia* sank just off Tillamook Rock. Bodies washed ashore at the base of Tillamook Head and were buried there by Jake Brallier, Jim Austin, and others. Government maps from 1876 and 1887 indicate a proposed lighthouse installation on Cape Falcon ("False Tillamook Head"). On June 8, 1866, President Andrew Johnson declared lands on False Tillamook Head a "lighthouse reservation." No lighthouse was constructed on the site.

A toll road, built by Clark Carnahan, Sam Adair, and Herbert Logan linked Cannon Beach with Seaside. John Antone Fastabend, with a nudge from the lumber tycoon Simon Benson, began constructing "cigar rafts" for towing timber along the Pacific Coast. Fastabend created enormous cradles containing bundles of chained logs one hundred to one hundred fifty feet long. The enormous rafts, nine hundred feet long, contained ten million board feet of lumber and drew thirty feet of water. The first raft ever to cross the Columbia River Bar ran amok and separated. A certain Mr. Bills, an early practitioner of beach combed scavenging, salvaged logs from the beach here and constructed the Bills Hotel. Versions of the old hotel have rested on the grounds of the Cannon Beach Conference Center to this day. As a historical footnote, William Jennings Bryant stayed in room 10 in 1904.

Cannon Beach Hotel, formerly Bills Hotel (Cannon Beach Conference Center Collection)

Mercantile stores catered to local needs, the two earliest being Sheets' and Lanphere's in the heart of downtown Cannon Beach. By 1910, a 504-foot trestle bridge spanned Elk Creek. A simple, planked, one-lane affair, horses and vehicles could cross the creek without fording. The bridge crossed just east of the location of the current bridge and disbursed bridge traffic onto the north end of Beaver Avenue. Several dozen cottages and residences straddled Hemlock Street in the presidential streets.

Camp 2-B, Necanicum River operation, US Army Spruce Production Division #9, east of existing Highway 26/101 junction (Clatsop County Historical Society)

Chapter 3
The First World War and Logging in Cannon Beach

As America engaged in the First World War, Cannon Beach and adjacent environs supplied vital spruce logs for the military's naval and aeronautical needs. Tracts east of Cannon Beach were designated military reserves. The US Army Spruce Production Division #9 began extracting valuable stands of spruce timber from the foothills surrounding the township. Les Ordway's father worked on crews harvesting timber on Tillamook Head. Located just south of Jasper Hovgaard's small dairy farm at the current Cannon Beach Junction, Crown-Willamette Paper Company's small railway trunk lines shunted out from their roundhouse and extended into previously inaccessible areas to remove the

Camp 2-B, Necanicum River operation, US Army Spruce Production Division #9, east of existing Highway 26/101 junction (Clatsop County Historical Society)

giant logs. The town's first mill sat at the foot of what is now Sunset Boulevard. Huge one-log loads—only the finest towering spruce specimens, ten growth rings to the inch—fell in the area that is now Spruce Park. A steam donkey yarded sawlogs from an area just east of the current Tolovana Wayside—the first "logging show" in town. A portable sawmill processed the logs at this location. With huge cross-cut saws, springboards, wedges, axes, cables, sweat, and steam, the finest stands of native Sitka spruce ever to appear on earth gradually fell and were trundled off to purposes military and commercial. In the earliest days of logging (Paul Bartels referred to them as "the bow and arrow days"), 106-foot logs inched through standing timber to provide the raw material for structures like the marvelous Forestry Building in Portland and the Warren Hotel in Tolovana Park.

The Warren Hotel

The Warren Hotel sat oceanfront, on a small knoll at the present site of Mo's Restaurant. Crafted from enormous logs, the fine landmark occupied the site until the early 1970s when it was razed. Paul Bartels constructed its vast beach-rock fireplace. Paul built virtually every fireplace in Cannon Beach for decades. Long a showpiece at the coast, many early residents

Interior of the Warren Hotel (Tom Olsen Collection)

attest to its charm and rustic splendor. Don Osborne's father recalls visiting it as a child with his grandfather, Frank Brallier. "We delivered milk there. It was a beautiful building.... I figured the people who stayed there must have been very wealthy." Finished in 1912, Governor Oswald West was the first person to sign the guest register.

Chapter 4
Car Camps, Cottages, and Moonshine

Tent camps at the Ecola Inn (Stevens Collection)

With the establishment of car camps and cottages, Cannon Beach and the Tolovana Park area commenced catering to visitors and people summering at the coast. A dance hall, later the Waves Roller Rink, occupied the southwest corner of First Street and Hemlock. Cannon Beach had no bars. It did have a strong religious component, however. The Temperance Movement and the Anti-Saloon League lobbied successfully for Prohibition. Spirits, termed "Blue Ruin" by some, filtered into the community through circuitous channels. My mother recounted visits to a gentleman known as Billy "Whoops My Dear" who produced moonshine out on Hamlet Route.

Gene and Selby Stringham distilled palatable white lightning for local trade and distributed it to special customers. Ray Jacobs and Paul Bartels served as delivery boys for this product. Elevated wooden boardwalks carried pedestrians across marshy sections of downtown Hemlock Street. Ray and Paul ran a regular route from the Stringham's stills to the boardwalks. At an appointed time, they deposited bottles under certain loose boards, caching the stored liquor for thirsty patrons. Milk bottles, painted white inside to fool the authorities, also appeared on select porches in the guise of dairy products.

Several informants describe clandestine liquor-running activities. Will and Mark Warren reportedly engaged in rum-running off the coastline, rendezvousing with vessels outside the territorial limit and ferrying liquor back to Smuggler's Cove at Short Sands, then hauling the bootlegged beverage north across Arch Cape to Cannon Beach. Leonard Gerritse Jr. relates an incident that occurred to his father during the prohibition era. Leonard Sr. visited Ray Jacobs one day. Ray lived in a shack behind what became Mac McCoy's service station. Leonard spotted a filled cup on a windowsill in the cabin. Given Ray's inclinations, Leonard assumed that the cup contained moonshine and hastily gulped the contents down. Ray returned to find the gasping Leonard outside his shack. The contents proved to be muriatic acid.

I met Ray Jacobs in the 1960s. Ray liked a sip and a good story. He confessed to an aversion to indoor plumbing. "Can't quite get used to those contraptions," he confided. A stocky, pleasantly trollish gent, he generally sported several days' stubble, an old Mackinaw jacket, tin pants, and a green baseball cap. We called guys like Ray old "whisker biscuits." He was a good spitter. Ray had fossicked around the Gold Beach area hoping for a gold dust payoff. The pull of gold tugged at him all his life. He spent at least the last half of his life in Cannon Beach, scratching along in one small shack or another. In his late seventies, he occupied an old plank-board shed on Sitka Street. A metal hospital bed, one bare light bulb, a perpetually perking coffee pot, a wood stove that provided heat for both comfort and cooking—these were Ray's amenities.

Ray enjoyed company, but he could also tolerate solitude better than most. He had done considerable oddjobbing. Before public works departments and other municipal improvements, Ray tended to the ditches and drainage areas adjacent to local roads. Hired by the state, Ray patrolled the roads with a wheelbarrow and shovel, unclogging blockages and maintaining drains. Ray also harvested game and sold it to local buyers and the Warren and Cannon Beach Hotels. Ray and Paul Bartels hiked into Indian Beach and Chapman Beach on low tides for clam harvest. They would cut the tops from tin milk jugs, fasten straps to the jugs, and

Ocean front beach cabins (Clatsop County Historical Society)

carry them to the beach on their shoulders. On decent low tides, an abundant razor clam catch filled the jugs to overflowing. They hiked back to town and sold the catch.

Les Ordway Stories

One of my best informants and a longtime friend is Lester Ordway. From a historical perspective, Les's lineage has unique roots in our area. Sergeant John Ordway of the Lewis and Clark Expedition was Les's early ancestor. Sergeant Ordway commanded the men of the expedition and controlled the parties under orders from Captains Lewis and Clark. His journal logs remain an integral part of the documentation pertaining to the exploration and reconnaissance of the western lands. His accounts of the cross-country journey flesh out those of his superiors in important ways.

Les Ordway is a wiry gentleman of scratch and vinegar. His contributions to our village are considerable, his memory keen and insightful. I recall Les as a local garage owner and mechanic who serviced our family cars, towed vehicles from the soft sand, and groomed young lads for the world of work in his tidy service station. Sometimes when you took your car to Les with a mechanical problem, he would act like he'd loaned you his car and you'd mistreated it severely. "Dammit, Pete, you've forgotten to change the oil in time! You'll ruin this car if you're not careful." Les had endearing crustiness. He expected high levels of responsibility and attention.

Les had little time for people who hay-wired mufflers to their cars or scrimped on maintenance. In one of my early encounters with Les, I got shamefacedly castigated for altering the family car. Terry Swigart and I had heated the front coil springs on our family's '53 Mercury convertible to "lower" or "rake" the front end—a very stylish thing for teenagers in the 1950s. My dad drove the car down the street, bouncing and thumping in the seat in tooth-jarring fashion. Detecting something amiss, he drove straight to Les's old service station. Les quickly discerned the problem and ordered my father to drag me down to the station.

I received a humiliating lecture of the head-hanging variety. "Damn, son, you've ruined the camber and caster of this fine car. What were you thinking? This car is too dangerous to drive now. Don't ever mess with the engineering of an automobile!" I remember Les replacing the coils in the front with extra-heavy springs just to teach me a lesson. After that the car actually rode higher in the front than it did formerly. I was the laughingstock of the high school parking lot. As the years passed and I got to know Les better, I began to suspect he would have done the same thing in his youth. He has strong spirit and an adventurous bent. I would say he's virtually done it all. I salute him and his kind. In these soft times they are an example we might all follow.

When you attend a dramatic presentation at the Coaster Theater, glance down at the floor in front of

Les Ordway (Laws Collection)

Les Ordway's gas station (Laws Collection)

Les Ordway and his buddy next to Bad Boy (Laws Collection)

its stage. Les and his helper installed the fine maple flooring that provided a smooth skating surface for generations of roller skaters at the Waves Rink. He and Duncan Shields installed the first street lights in Cannon Beach. The lights ran from dusk to about eleven at night in the thirties. As a former dory fisherman, I have long revered Les Ordway for his pluck and skills as a doryman. The Cannon Beach Historical Society has pictures of Les's first boat, the Bad Boy. Approximately twelve feet long, crafted of spruce boards, the Bad Boy had almost no freeboard. Les rowed the tiny dory through the surf and into the open sea regularly. One photo shows Les as a young man standing next to the slender vessel on the beach. The gunwales come to just below his knees.

"Did you ever take that out to the lighthouse?" I once asked him.

"Oh, sure," he told me grinning, "dozens of times."

"Did you ever take it onto Tillamook Rock [Tillamook Rock Lighthouse is three miles offshore from Cannon Beach]?"

"Of course, we always took it onto the rock. The lighthouse keepers loved to see us. They got lonely out there and enjoyed the company. And, man, could they cook! Didn't have anything else to do out there, I guess. Their pastries and pies were delicious!"

"Ah, Pete, in the early days we'd row out there on a good morning, find a spot to drop our gear, and the salmon, big silvers, they were thick. You could work just outside the surf line off Seaside and catch big Chinook. That was some fishing."

Les and Jim Hickle launched from The Needles in their double-ended dory late into the 1970s, rowing through the surf the old way, firing up the motor-welled outboard when they got outside.

A single log load, Van Vleet Logging Company, 1950s (Amos Collection)

Les told me about his logging experience and the chronology of the timber harvest:

The first job I had was "spark chaser" on a landing. The steam donkeys in those days threw off clouds of embers. When the humidity dropped, they could ignite chips and cause a fire. I raced around the donkey landing with wet burlap sacks extinguishing the fires. Boy, those things could really heat up with a good load of hemlock wood in the firebox. We used fire, though, to burn up the waste logs. I worked on the Warren Hotel and we burned logs constantly. We drilled holes and put the embers in holes to slowly eliminate logs that were in the way.

A man and a Sitka spruce log (Amos Collection)

The first logging was in Spruce Park. That was the only logging in Cannon Beach for some time. Huge trees covered the rest of the land, right down to the beach itself. Not much undergrowth, either. The next logging was done by Kenny Cahill up in that bottom-land by the Elk Creek Forks. A guy named Habecost followed next. Van Vleet started in the late 1930s. I tried to get on there, but George Van Vleet told me he had guys lined up deep trying to get in.

We reminisced for a bit about the arduous nature of the work itself. Fallers chopped and sawed the massive spruce above the lower butts of the trees; they perched on springboards notched into the tree trunks.

"Drag saws bucked up the fallen logs on the ground. They were powered by a simple two-cycle engine. A flywheel and sprocket system pushed and pulled the blade back and forth through the log. It oscillated to make the cutting easier. We cut up most of the logs with them."

I mentioned Mary "Ma" Gerritse to him. "I'll tell you one thing about that gal, when she told you something, you could take it to the bank!"

Paul Bartels

Paul Bartels plied his masonry trades in the village for decades. As a young man, he hunted game to supply meat for the hotels, chopped wood for stoves and hotel fireplaces, foraged for shellfish and salmon. Clients arriving by stage from Seaside found Paul waiting to ferry them across Elk Creek to the Cannon Beach Hotel. Paul, like Les, was a jack-of-all-trades. In his later working life, he specialized in beach-rock chimneys and fireplaces. Landmark buildings and most early residences boasted a Bartels chimney. The Warren Hotel, the Cannon Beach Hotel, Newman's Drug Store, and the Log Cabin Restaurant (Paul built the restaurant for his sister Marie in the 1920s), all displayed fine examples of his craft.

In 1955 my father built our home on Laurel Street. After some cajoling, Paul agreed to build our chimney and fireplace. Paul, then in his early eighties, arrived to survey the project. A slim man, slightly stooped from years of labor, he arrived bundled in an old red wool

Paul Bartels constructing a chimney at the Sketch Pad (Lackaff Collection)

coat and surveyed the task at hand. He spoke softly and with deliberate consideration, a man of gentle smiles and humor.

My father threw some numbers and a blueprint at him. "I figured the mantel ought to be about five feet ten inches off the floor, the opening about six feet four inches wide. What do you think, Paul?"

"Harvey," he responded in his wry fashion, "those numbers all sound well and good, but I don't work much in numbers. I never got the handle of figuring. Let's just lay some of these bricks on the floor and look at it. I cipher these fireplaces out at so many bricks wide, so many tall. It works best for me."

I watched, rapt, for two days as Paul methodically fashioned our grand fireplace. He worked by feel and intuition, cautiously buttering the bricks and massaging them into place. The final product could easily grace the finest Colonial residences of early Massachusetts. A drive through the streets of Cannon Beach still gives evidence of his mastery today.

Hemlock Street, looking south, 1920s (Grant/Bartl Collection)

Chapter 5

The Twenties and Thirties

Between the wars, many changes occurred in Cannon Beach. The Depression touched the town, and some hard feelings lingered. One resident who protested in his own small way dwelt in a one-room shack on the upper reaches of Arch Cape Creek. Ed "Smitty" Smith, a local character, carved out a cleared area and constructed his habitation. Proximal to his shack was a fine truck garden. Ed eked out an existence doing chores, handy manning, and poaching. Elk and deer ravaged his vegetable gardens on a regular basis. Ed responded with force, eating the offenders and burying their carcasses for fertilizer. Leonard Gerritse Jr. recounts visits to Ed's place in the thirties: "His privy had a regular toilet seat, and when you lifted the lid, he had fastened a full-size newspaper photo of Herbert Hoover on it! His comment was, 'It makes me feel good to have him kiss my—every time I go.'"

Some goings on about town in the 1920s and 1930s: The Civilian Conservation Corps (CCC) boys rolled in to tidy up what would ultimately become Ecola State Park. Barracks housing the young men sat about seven miles east of the Cannon Beach Junction, at the current location of the Suppe place on Highway 26. The CCC brought city lads into the area to engage in various projects in the great outdoors. Some of the locals viewed the Corps' job skills with mild disdain. A few old woods colts scoffed openly at the puny Caterpillar tractor the Corps brought along for yarding stumps, a D-5 to do a D-8 job, if you will. Formerly in private hands, the people of the State of Oregon received the park property through a generous bequest. The Chapmans owned the point that now bears their name; the Flanders, Glisan, and Lewis families owned the land to the north. Roads had been maintained on these properties by the Gerritse family before the land's donation to the State of Oregon. Following state acquisition, the CCC constructed picnic facilities in the new park site, along with trails and benches. One researcher at the Clatsop County Historical Society credits the CCC with introducing opossums to the area. He claimed the workers favored them for food. I'm skeptical, but open to conclusive evidence.

Falcon Cove Development

The Kruschke Brothers, Ed and Bill, commenced gouging out acreage at Falcon Cove, quarrying and constructing roads. The Gerritses, who seem almost omnipresent in those times, helped them. Folks called Bill Kruschke "the Hermit of Falcon Cove." A reclusive sort, Bill manufactured handmade cigars in his dwelling south of Arch Cape. He occupied a house constructed of driftwood material scavenged from the beach.

George Shields remembers Bill's jaunts to Astoria to sell his quality cigars: "About every two weeks Bill would pack up his hand-rolled cigars and hike up to the Warren Hotel. He'd spend the night and then walk or take the bus to Astoria. After a few days he'd return to the hotel, take a meal, pick up a few supplies at the store, bacon, beans and so forth, and head back down there. No one else lived in those parts then. He was pretty much by himself."

Elk Creek Bridge

A footbridge was constructed for pedestrians across Elk Creek that linked Spruce Street with the Price's Campground on the north edge of the stream. In the winter months the dismantled bridge was taken down and stored to avoid damage. Brown's Service Station appeared on the south

Top: *First bridge over Elk Creek, 1920s (Clatsop County Historical Society)* **Bottom:** *Warren Auto Campground (Clatsop County Historical Society)*

end of the Elk Creek Bridge. John Gerritse built a substantial garage at the location of the present Driftwood Inn. Bert Blake operated the garage for many years. A hall for community gatherings sat on the northeast corner of the current Conference Center grounds.

The Warren Brothers set about filling the swampy land north of the Warren Hotel and established the Warren Auto Campground. Clearing away huge spruce trees, the brothers and their help built two-by-four platforms with low walls that provided a base for canvas tarpaulins. Car campers occupied the campsites in the summer months. A surprisingly large number of current homes began life as either tent platforms or small loggers' cabins. My brother Tim and I remodeled one of these structures a decade ago. Tearing away at shingles and framing, we stripped the building down to its bare bones, an old tent platform and appended sun deck.

Hemlock Street, looking north, 1930s (Stevens Collection)

The Cannon Beach Water Systems

Every residence and development required a waterworks. Frank Brallier had one that served his Wave Crest development. The Mansurs and Settums had another. The Andersons, Warrens, Woodfields, and others all established tanks and piping in Tolovana Park. First a Mr. White—later a man named McKay (pronounced McEye)—supplied water to Cannon Beach from a spring east of town.

Cedar piping, formed of cedar staving and wrapped together with wire, carried the water from the springs to town along what came to be known locally as "the Pipeline Trail." The pipes looked like giant cane fly rods in cross-section. The trail and pipeline headed east from the town on Monroe Street, passed through what is now the RV Park, and followed the Elk Creek Road to the water source located, then and now, above the West Fork of Elk Creek.

When the Leonard Gerritses, Junior and Senior, contracted for stump removal on the presidential streets, Adams to Van Buren, enormous spruce hulk remnants dotted the residential streets. The Gerritse family owned the first beefy Caterpillar and was hired to clear the offending stumpage. Grubbing out the root wads, the Cat blade occasionally hooked a length of wood pipe in the street. A geyser flume jetting into the sky signaled a burst pipe. The men would clear the area surrounding the break, chop a clean hole in the cedar pipe, and chink the damaged area with a stob of wood. Leonard Jr. remembers his father hunkered in a ditch—water spraying everywhere and drenching the poor man—pounding a chunk of

Bathers in Elk Creek (Lindsey Collection)

wood into the line with a hatchet. The process was repeated a discouraging number of times.

Recreation in the Twenties and Thirties

Physical culture became popular in America. Many resorts catered to an increasingly mobile population that toured to seaside destinations. Cannon Beach and other resort towns provided natatoriums, an indoor alternative to surf swimming and bathing. Natationists, swimmers in layman's terms, frolicked in pools that contained heated salt water. Seaside, Rockaway, and Cannon Beach all had fine examples that operated well into the 1960s. Penny arcades, trinkets, cotton candy, popcorn, and taffy characterized the commercial offerings at these recreation centers. Our "nat" sat just south of Whale Park. Billy Mahon constructed the building, extracting water from nearby Elk Creek to fill his indoor pool. Dances and socializing took place upstairs in a large hall. During summer months,

Duck Pin Cafe (D. Johnson collection)

movie projectors trained on the south wall cast images on the building. Captain Midnight serials claimed the attention of delighted moviegoers.

Ray Walker created his roller skating rink, The Waves, since reconstructed as the Coaster Theatre. Families haunted the rink on summer nights, circling to polka tunes and waltzes. Mr. Walker opened on inclement afternoons during the summer, an altogether too frequent occurrence. Restless children, bored and cabin-bound, found the rink an oasis of joy during sodden summers. The Jacobsens owned a bowling alley across Hemlock Street. Bowlers rolled cricket-sized balls at "duck pins," stumpy dwarf-sized pins hand set by generations of summer teens. After the building burned in the 1960s, many of the pins found favor with cedar-bolt splitters who used the pins as clubs to whack froes, splitting shake bolts into cedar shakes and shingles.

Children—my mother and her sister among them—virtually lived at William Spaulding's Elk Creek Riding Academy. Spaulding had horses for hire that could be rented for seventy-five cents an hour and coursed along the beaches and into the hills behind. Regular night rides to Silver Point, complete with wiener roasts and bonfires, established a tradition that exists today with the Swigart's Sea Ranch.

Auntie Mansur and the Road to Cannon Beach

The road between Cannon Beach and Seaside improved somewhat, although its one hundred and eleven curves tested the mettle of generations of automobile drivers. George Shields likes to tell his story about

Cannon Beach Stage car (Lindsey Collection)

Mrs. Mansur—"Auntie Mansur" —and her trips across the road. The Frye family lived on the north side of Elk Creek above the bridge in the Stamm's house. George describes the large family as somewhat threadbare: "The kids wore the same overalls to school every day." George, Bernie Frye, and Snookie Becker were the only three students in the first grade at Cannon Beach School. The Frye family had no automobile. Old Man Frye was exceptionally hard of hearing and carried a length of old rubber hose with a funnel on the end for an ear trumpet.

One day Auntie Mansur picked up Mr. Frye on the road at Seaside on her way to Cannon Beach. Auntie's driving atrocities were legendary. Speed and inattention both played a role. Seated behind the wheel of her '37 Chev Roadster, she cut a wide and wicked swath. As the hurtling roadster careened down the slope toward Cannon Beach, Frye, terrified, hauled out his makeshift ear trumpet in order to converse with Auntie and express his fears. Auntie Mansur mistook the hose for a gun barrel and panicked, augering the roadster into an embankment.

A motor stage retrieved passengers from Seaside, many of whom came from the railway station during summer months, and transported them to Cannon Beach. O. B. Cole operated this vehicle. I have in my collection a photo of this machine, a veritable motorized pack animal with luggage and trunks strapped to its fenders and roof. Mr. Cole was appointed postmaster in the early days.

George Shields and the BB Gun

George Shields dug into his memory bag for me one evening and spoke of his early childhood:

"As a kid around here, you couldn't get into too much trouble 'cause everyone knew you. Well, my dad gave me a BB gun. One day me and Bernie Frye were shooting that BB gun down in the willow marsh by the Warren Campground. My old black dog was with us. Two old spinster schoolteachers, the Butler sisters, walked by near us. I plinked a couple of shots at them and stung one of them right in the backside. They immediately lit off for my house and we ran off and hid.

When I got home, my dad gave me a terrible licking and bent the BB gun in two over his knee. When the Butler girls told my dad that two boys with a black dog had shot them with a BB gun, he didn't have to look far to find the culprits."

A boy had freedom to roam and explore barely tamed country. George told me:

I trapped on Warren Creek [site of the Tolovana Wayside]. Bill Eames, an old Indian, taught me how to trap muskrat. I bought spring traps from Sears Roebuck. I sold the skins in the mail order catalog too. My line ran along the creek up into the hills. Every morning before school, I'd check the lines, then run them again after school with a kerosene lamp for light. Didn't get beaver, but I trapped a lot of muskrats.

George described a few characters he remembered:

George and Norma Smith ran a little store at the corner of Tanana and Hemlock. You know, Pete, at Adelhart's place there. George did odd jobs and a lot of drinking. He had an old pickup with the back end cut off. He and Jim Ellis would get to drinkin' and carrying on whenever he got a little cash. The two of them would "jungle up" in one of those little tent platform buildings down at the Warren Campground, playing cards and raising hell. Sometimes, even in the middle of the winter. It was not unusual to see George come home after a spree and see his wife Norma chase him around the neighborhood with a two-by-four. I remember one morning George and Jim began digging a septic tank hole; some idea caught their fancy and they drifted off. When they came back, Norma was down in the hole quietly digging. "I've got her where I want her now!" says George, "Go ahead and throw dirt on her and bury her!" They were a rough lot.

Chickens and Wild Animal Stories

The Cannon Beach Library and Women's Club staged benefits to fund book purchases for its facility. One interesting account describes its annual "Chicken Fricassee Dinner." Louise Bartels, Doris Stringham, and Myrtle Grailer supervised the preparation of an elaborate chicken dinner each year that supplemented the library fund. Every spring Louise Bartels would cull out old hens to donate for the supper. The sacrificed hens did their small part to increase literacy. Governor Oswald West had established his substantial log residence above the beach south of Haystack Rock in 1913. West had a pet bobcat. One spring just prior to the benefit, Louise heard a ruckus in the hen house. West's cat, strayed from the family home, had commenced to threaten the very future of literary culture in the City of Cannon Beach! Louise dispatched

Cannon Beach Library, south side of Second Street (Cannon Beach Library Collection)

Top: *Oswald West house (Tom Olsen Collection)* **Bottom:** *Warren Hotel (Tom Olsen Collection)*

him with a single shot.

Chickens suffered additional humiliation in those days long past. The Warrens kept a pet monkey on premises at the Warren Hotel. He had watched Edra Warren pluck chickens in preparation for hotel banquets. "Monkey see . . . ," well, you know the rest. That old monkey occasionally shagged an unwary chicken up a tall tree on the hotel grounds and commenced plucking the protesting bird's plumage! Guests reveled in the fowl's discomfiture.

Chapter 6
Cannon Beach During World War II

Following the events of December 7th, 1941, the residents of coastal Oregon properly intensified their vigilance. From the distance of our perspective now, we can scarcely imagine the quailed hearts of the townspeople in that time. Living in isolation on a scantily populated coastline, the threat from air and sea was far too real. The only instances in modern times of aggressors penetrating our continental borders occurred along the coast of Oregon during that era. Incendiary balloons sent into the jet stream plummeted to earth and ignited stands of timber. Japanese aircraft breached coastal security and jettisoned firebombs in south coast timber. One submarine-launched Japanese torpedo ground ashore at Clatsop beach. Fears were certainly not unfounded.

Shore batteries, blimp surveillance, establishment of an observation bunker on Tillamook Head, all evidenced an intensified coastal defensive posture. Civilian defense groups manned small buildings approximately eight feet wide that sheltered shore-side observers. Affixed to the ceilings of those buildings were aircraft silhouettes enabling observers to identify aircraft. Strict rules regarding light discipline prevailed. Residents installed blackout curtains on cabin windows. Automobiles travelling at night did so with no headlights, or with only very small lights reminiscent of the old "dark lanterns." National and local security reached a pitch difficult to appreciate in our day and time. First the Army National Guard and later Coast Guard equestrian units patrolled the beaches and headlands, combing desolate strands for enemy inter-

Coast Guard housing built during World War II, building on the left (Cannon Beach Conference Center Collection

lopers. Only the most steadfast and rigorous souls attempted the drive from Seaside to Cannon Beach over the road of 111 sinuous curves during blackouts!

George Shields recalls the Christmas of 1941 with clarity. A merchant marine vessel bound overseas foundered at the mouth of the Columbia River. Laden with Christmas goods, the ship's cargo drifted ashore on local beaches and strew the sands at Chapman Beach with merchandise sufficient to stock department stores. Turkeys, fur coats, Christmas trees, toys, watches, and jewelry comprised the flotsam. Covered with a viscous oil coating, much remained unsalvageable.

Tension characterized that holiday. The Shields family shared Christmas with the Mansurs and Settums every year. On that Christmas Eve in 1941, the Shields family drove to the Mansur's home at Silver Point. They parked at the Mansur garage which sat beside the roadway above the point. A narrow trail dropped down to the Mansur house, situated about one quarter mile below. The family gathered up Christmas gifts and descended to the house. Duncan Shields (George's father) carried a flashlight to illuminate the slippery trail in the darkness. Suddenly a voice challenged them: "Halt!" Terrified, the Shields family stopped in the trail. Men with raised rifles held them at bay. An Army National Guard officer proceeded to interrogate them.

"Where are you going?"

"To the Mansur House."

"Do you know those people?"

"Of course," Mr. Shields responded, "we've known them for years."

"I'll escort you to the house for purposes of identification," the officer told them.

Reaching the front door, the officer knocked. Mr. Mansur, known as "Uncle" to the Shieldses, appeared.

"Can you identify these people?"

"Never seen them before in my life," Uncle responded, grinning a sly-dog grin.

Chapter 7
Summering in Cannon Beach After WWII

My first encounter with Cannon Beach occurred in 1946. Our family summered in Cannon Beach, travelling by train from San Francisco to Portland and thence to the coast via the old highway. I was just a slip of a youth then, but I recall impressions. Families spent several months or weeks at cottages on an annual basis. One would inquire of the postmaster or postmistress, "Have the Evansons arrived yet? Have the Reeds shown up this year?" Even in mid-August, the heart of summer, the township exuded a sleepy quality. Day tripping was impossible.

My family lived on the beach during daylight hours, lizarding away the hours in sunshine, exploring trails and quiet beaches, harvesting wild strawberries, raking Dungeness crabs from pools at low tide, strolling quiet streets to pick up a loaf of fresh bread before dinner. Elevated boardwalks fronted stores on Hemlock Street. Tidal flow, even in the summer months, swirled several feet of brackish water beneath a pedestrian's feet at high tide. Red-winged blackbirds perched in willow branches near the bakery and fish market. Wild band-tailed pigeons flustered in the branches of grand, silvered snags near the main street.

High Waters on Hemlock Street (Stevens Collection)

AMUSEMENTS

PENNY ARCADE
"Fun for All—
　　　　All for Fun"
NEXT TO BOWLING ALLEY

AQUARIUM

Visit the
SEASIDE AQUARIUM
Live Octopus Sea Anemonies
Many other Deep Sea Wonders
SEASIDE, ORE.

ATTORNEYS

IRVING C. ALLEN
ATTORNEY AT LAW
City Attorney　　　City Hall
Telephone 380. Residence 208
SEASIDE, OREGON

AUTO CAMPS

HYDRO GAS EQUIPPED MODERN
COTTAGES
DRIFTWOOD CAMP GROUND
North Side of Elk Creek
Camping　Picnics　Trailers
MR. & MRS. G. M. ZIMMERMAN
Cannon Beach, Ore.

AUTO FREIGHT

NEHALEM VALLEY MOTOR FREIGHT
Portland　　Vernonia　　Seaside
Ph. Ea. 1522　　1042　　　84
Cannon Beach
84

AUTO REPAIRING

AAA Mechanical Repairing
Shell Products
GREER'S SERVICE
R. J. GREER, Manager

Gas - Oil - Parts and Accessories
Greasing - Repairing - Towing
Phone 701-J-12　Cannon Beach, Ore.

BAKERIES

CANNON BEACH BAKERY
Large variety fresh sliced bread every day.

BARBER SHOP

RED'S BARBER SHOP
Near Cannon Beach P. O.

BEAUTY SHOP

BOB SHOPPE
CHRISTOL & DOROTHEA

Phone 350
212 Broadway　　Seaside, Oregon

ABBREVIATIONS

O. C. H.—Oregon Coast Highway.
O. F.—Ocean Front.
E.—East of Oregon Coast Highway.
W.—West of Oregon Coast Highway.
NR.—Near.
M. P.—Mile Post.

If you wish friends to find you, introduce yourself to the nearest information depot.

1. Driftwood Camp.
2. Coles C. B. Merc. & Bus Depot.
3. Burrows News Stand.
4. Ecola Inn.
5. George's Grocery.
6. Shield's Grocery.
7. Charles Hotel.
8. White's Grocery.

COTTAGE NAMES

A

A-Flat, Umpqua St.—7
Agaming, O. F., N. of Brallier Rd.—7
Agate Shop Cottages, O. C. H. & 2nd—2
Alma Cottage, N. of Ecola Inn—4
Antler Lodge, 3rd & Hemlock—2
Arcadia Cottages, 1½ Mi. So. Charles Hotel—7
Arden Villa, Spruce St.—2
Astoria, First St.—2
Athlone, East Adams St.—2
Avalon, Fir St.—2

B

Bank's Pike, W. Wash.—2-3
Beach View, Btw. 4th & 5th on Fir—1
Belmor, O. F. N. of Ecola Inn—4
Beverly, East Jackson St.—2
B-Flat, Umpqua St.—7
Bide-A-Wee, O. F. and Siuslaw—7
Billikins, Skans,—4
Bird Rock, Fir St. Mc D.—2
Blinkem, George's Groc.—5
Blue Bird, O. F. Nic'l.—2
Blue Jay, Arcadia—7
Blue Jay, East Van Buren St.—4
Blue Seas, 2nd St. Haynes—2
Bonnie Nook, E. Monroe—2
Breeze-Inn, Lagasses—5
Briar-Cot, E. Madison—2-3
Brownie, Hiway near 3rd St.—2
Burrow-Inn, E. Wash.—2

C

Campbell's Lodge, 1 bl. So. Brallier Rd.—7
Cap Johnson's Cottages, Surf Crest—6
Care-Free. Hosbon's St.—5
"Carol" Cottage. W. Jefferson St.—2
Cedar Lodge, 5th St.—2
Charles Cottages, Brallier Rd.—7
Clarks, Taft St.—2
Cole's Cott., W. Wash.—2

Cannon Beach Directory 1941-42 (H. Johnson Collection)

Typical Cannon Beach cottage (Cannon Beach Conference Center Collection)

Cannon Beach was a cottage town. Graying, shingled structures stumbled down graveled lanes. One knew almost everyone. Summer families weren't strangers, only expected arrivals, like the swallows of Capistrano. Walking the streets or boardwalks, people waved at passersby or stopped to exchange pleasantries. In that halcyon time—a term particularly apt considering its relationship to the mythical kingfisher that quieted turbulence—one swam in a living dream of experience, an idyll, a waking trance of cerulean blues, whites, and greens. Armies of spruce, cedar, and hemlock marched from the foothills behind town and down to the sea on capes and headlands; the town itself was set like some precious stone in a green band of mountains.

Wood heated most residences. Our rented cottage contained a wood stove. All meals required firing that wood stove with split fir housed in a shack behind the house. By simply closing my eyes I can slip back into that woodshed in a trice. Opening the plank doors, boy wonders revealed themselves to my young eyes. Cord upon cord of old growth fir exuded a heady resinous flavor to a mushroomy air. That smell so characteristic of intermittently occupied beach structures nearly bowled me over. Old hemp twine wrapped bamboo surf rods hung in hooks on the walls, sharing quarters with crab rings, rusted, stumpy shovels for digging razor clams, peaveys, mauls, glistening axes, kerosene lanterns, oars, tin pails, and hand tools. We split wood prodigiously, stoking the stove's hungry maw at every meal. My father let me help, deftly placing a bolt of fir on the chopping block and judiciously whisking his hand free as I sliced toward the block.

We favored seafood. Nate Cozey, owner of the cabin, frequented the offshore rocks, often fishing through tides at Haystack Rock and Chapman Point, returning at dark with sacks of surfperch and greenling. On extremely low tides, I joined my mother in tide pools and assisted her as she waded breast deep in the water, raking crab from the base of deep holes with a long-pronged rake. The abundance of shellfish in those times is scarcely imaginable. We feasted like lords on razor clams and crab. A savory berry pie, wild blue huckleberry by choice, capped these occasions. On extraordinary days, a few pieces of Tom n' Larry's incomparable fudge or English toffee finished the meal.

Cannon Beach, as it has been for so many families before and since, was a summer dream, a chance to escape the hurly-burly of our other lives, the cares of city living and its tensions. We were soon to experience its other aspect, a small village of frequently turbulent seasons, perched like a tenacious barnacle on a raw stretch of the Oregon coast.

Chapter 8

Settling in Cannon Beach in the Early Fifties

My family settled permanently in Cannon Beach in 1953. We moved from San Francisco smack in the heart of a full storm that January. As we drove up the coastline, huge white scuffs skidded across the road-bed. In our naiveté, we thought the white material was snow! The blown drifts proved to be sea foam churned up from the shoreline below.

Wintering in that year revealed many surprises. Year-round residents numbered 106 according to census figures. Most wage earners worked in tim-ber-extracting jobs. The harsh climate surprised us. I shivered for the better part of six months before grad-ually acclimatizing.

Going to School

A school bus ferried all high school students to Seaside. On my first ride to school, the sheer physical magni-tude of my male schoolmates shook my confidence drastically. Sons of loggers and outdoorsmen, these teens, many of stout Scandinavian stock, towered over me, full-muscled men in schoolboy roles: Larry Rasmussen, seven foot two inches tall, 185 pounds; the Wright Brothers, Punk, Ron, Jim, none weighing in

Peter Lindsey and family, Cozy house, 1946 (Lindsey Collection)

under 200 pounds; Dennis Rittenback, six foot four; Bill Knight, the same. By the grace of the good Lord, they seemed convivial, even friendly! Most appeared attuned to the rigors of outdoor life, keen pursuers of fish, game, and physical exertion. We existed almost exclusively outdoors when not attending school, free to range at our hearts' content in deep woods, along the shoreline, in and around the creek and estuary.

Boy Stuff—Growing Up in Cannon Beach in the Fifties

Most of us owned guns, a shotgun or .22 caliber rifle. We hiked or waded incessantly, tracking, drawn by some memory, the scent of a spore blown on the winds of a time gone by. We shot and killed many things. Lazy grouse perched like chickens on an aged spruce, unfazed by our crackled footfalls in the orange alder leaves of October. A black bear, about our age and stature, doomed by blackberry madness, stumbled across our path into oblivion. We strapped his carcass to the hood of a '55 Chevrolet, much to our ignominy, and paraded him about town. Wild band-tailed pigeons ghosted through the skeletal spruce snags behind Newman's Drug Store. Canny and vigilant, these spooky fliers gorged on fermenting elderberry, casting caution to the wind. We shot them on the Fourth of July, the reports of the rifles masked by fireworks downtown. We thrashed through thickets of salal, eavesdropped on families of beaver and otter, and once glimpsed a cougar at twilight, twitching its tail to and fro on a rotted stump. We shinnied slender red alder, climbing until the trunks slumped like taught bows, splintering us plummeting to the ground below. For sport, we spotlighted raccoons in tall trees, goaded some young fool into climbing the tree with a gunnysack, and tried to capture the snarling beast. Terry Swigart had some measure of success in these adventures, if my memory serves me correctly.

Logging paraphernalia, rusting and decaying in the undergrowth, lay scattered and abandoned widely. Blocks, wire cable, oxidized crosscut saws, slumping spar trees, donkey engine skids, and collapsing powder sheds lay in our field of exploration. "The woods" were accessible to anyone and we took full advantage. For several years my buddy Gerry Sroufe and I hiked a regular route on an almost daily basis: up the Elk Creek Road (we called it the Night Ride Road because the Swigarts took their guided horse trips up the road every Friday and Saturday night in the summer months), right at the creek on the spur that led to the watershed, back on the Warren Road to Tolovana or north to the Sunset Hills, and back to town. We learned every turn on the trail, the habits of beast and fowl, the sound of grouse drumming in a dusty roadbed, the season of blackberries and wild huckleberries, red and blue, the acrid and caustic properties of wild cucumber pods.

Sometimes we discovered discarded or misplaced dynamite sticks and caps. Some of the chaps had practical dynamite experience. We put their savvy to use on powder experiments. How many sticks did it take to elevate a stump off the ground? Fortunately, we avoided the cataclysmic, but the aftermaths of explosions often took on unexpected and unanticipated magnificence. On one occasion we levitated a tree stump clean off the earth in Swigart's pasture and nearly placed it in orbit! Fragments rained down for an obscene length of time to our hoots and glee.

My arch-bosom crony Gerald Sroufe owned a fine green rowboat. Like Toad and Mole in *The Wind in the Willows*, we sported up and down the half-mile reach of Elk Creek, our stream of youthful memory, rowing like fiends from Hell.

"It's Sroufe," he would say leaning back on the oars, "not Sriff or Srowf or Syph. Sroufe. I don't know why people can't get it! S-R-O-U-F-E. If it ain't Sroufe, it ain't me!"

He had constructed a small docking area on Elk Creek just below tidewater. Other local boys had their watercraft on the creek as well, plying the stream up toward the forks, fishing, exploring, plundering. In the fifties, fine runs of silver and Chinook salmon returned and spawned in the gravel beds at its forks. Each fall blue backs and cutthroat trout entered tidewater and filtered upstream. We waited expectantly, poised and primed, trolling long red-feather spoons for a prized catch. During summer months we scavenged lures and weights from submerged logs and low branches, proud of our retrieved spoils. I have an indelibly etched map of that lower stream and its sloughs logged in my sensibilities since adolescence.

In early spring, when skunk cabbage probed its yellow stalks from the wetland bog and crows whirled and cavorted in the creek corridor, we of-

Gerald Sroufe, Peter Lindsey, and Tim Lindsey on Elk Creek in Gerald's rowboat, 1953 (Lindsey Collection)

ten set off on a preseason fishing campout. Armed with castoff Army surplus gear, cans of manure worms dislodged from Swigart's horse barn, an old pup tent from the then defunct Cub Scout Troop 776, cans of creamed corn, and Dinty Moore Beef Stew scrounged from Sroufe's Grocery, we strapped on our Packer John frame packs and tramped upstream to the headwaters. The official trout season generally opened at the end of May. We knew the fish to be particularly ravenous in April and early May. Besides, the illegal nature of our junkets added to the titillation and adventure. We took no poles, only small coils of line and leader. Fishing poles would be "evidence" if we got caught.

Our favorite campsite was at the falls, down at the end of Burn Road. We loved chopping things. Scores of alder thickets probably still bear the scars of our hewing. After establishing camp, we selected a few promising alder switches and flensed the soft bark and limbs from a four to five foot wand. Carefully applying line and leader, we inched our way to a pool and tested the waters. Usually several greedy trout filled our bag. Sroufie seared up a pot of Dinty Moore Beef Stew heated over a blazing bed of alder switches. Sometimes we cooked the trout in the stew pot,

Peter Lindsey and Gerald Sroufe on their Pop Franklin bicycles, 1953 (Lindsey Collection)

eyeballs, fins, and all. On other occasions, we staked them Indian fashion on green sticks. Sweet alder smoke rose, trembling the new growth, the pale lemon-green alder leaves in the creek bottom. We capped the meal with liberal doses of oatmeal cookies and saltwater taffy. Later, we lagged rocks, bragged and storied, drifted in a reverie of water motion and stream narcosis.

"Pops" at the Beach

Cannon Beach had its share of "Pops" in the early days; perhaps they existed in many rural small towns in a time now gone: Pop Shaeffer at the Arch Cape Union Station, Pop Wright at his campground at the foot of Sunset Hill, Pop Wagner in his small auto repair shop on east Jackson Street, Pop Franklin behind the Ecola Hotel in his bike shop. Earning "Pop" status in a community generally entailed certain recognized qualifications: a long-standing relationship with goings-on in the village, a pleasant demeanor and patience when dealing with younger people, certain unusual or idiosyncratic skills or trades. No Pops I knew were ever ogres or gruff goats. On the contrary, most of these venerable gentlemen had special

Travelling on the beach road around Hug Point (Tom Olsen Collection)

knowledge, a personal connection with the past, humor, and stories to whet the imagination of a young person.

Take Pop Franklin, for example. During my teens he operated a tiny bike repair and rental shop in the garage below his upstairs living quarters. All the bikes were one-speed, fat-tired, crusty veterans of countless beach excursions. Pop ran his bikes like a string of horses, rounding up old strays from neighborhood woodsheds and garages, cannibalizing parts from one to jury-rig another. Several generations of pre-car adolescents wheeled these instances of obscure morphogenesis around the gravel roads, trails, and beaches of Cannon Beach in the forties and fifties. Strange hermaphroditic blends of rusty male and female cyclery, these beasts carried us around town like faithful mules, quirky but generally reliable.

Pop had no new bikes. When some part failed or sand seized up a sprocket, you went to Pop's. Rubbaging around in the dark recesses of his garage, he located a tire tube for patching, a serviceable sprocket, a stray pedal. With a bicycle our range of exploration increased ten-fold. Somewhere in my collection of old photographs, I have a picture of Sroufie and me mounted on our Franklin bikes, two swainish lads affecting teenage maturity. On this occasion, we prepared for an overnight bike trek to the hinterlands, seven miles to a campout on Arch Cape Creek, our first overnight venture with no adult supervision. I recall a provisioning stop at Ethel Legault's Arch Cape Grocery to lay in a supply of beef stew and cookies.

The Beach as a Roadway, and the Towing Business

The sands of Cannon Beach served as a roadway from the 1880s until the late part of this century. Both horse-drawn and motorized vehicles fell prey to an inhospitable surf line and the shifting sands of its beach. Pioneer accounts indicate countless incidents of wagons being prized from soft sands and crab holes. Frank Brallier gained some notoriety for his Samaritan actions, extracting lodged vehicles with his team of horses. One account describes his efforts in wrenching a Model T Ford from the corpse of a stranded whale! In what must have been an embarrassing predicament, the motorist discovered himself run afoul on a mountain of whale flesh. Grandpa Brallier hitched his team and extricated the auto from a blubbery morass.

Towing has proven to be a profitable trade from the turn of the century to the present day. A man named Greer apparently operated the first towing vehicle. The Warren Brothers also owned an open-cab truck of some fashion, capable of removing mired vehicles. Leonard Gerritse Jr. described his father's early tow vehicle, a converted Lozier:

Although everyone used the beach as a highway as it was a lot better and smoother than the roads and had no mud holes, the access was only dependable where there were small creeks with a constant flow of water. This kept the sand hard enough for cars. There were only a few spots—the Ecola Inn, the Warren Hotel, and Arch Cape Creek—that had connecting ramps. My dad had a towing service along with his service station, and he told that quite a few motorists—after having him tow their cars out of the surf, crab holes, or whatever—would take off while he was stowing his tow gear and try to outrun him to avoid paying what they owed. Dad got tired of this after awhile and made a tow car out of his Lozier. This outfit would run rings around the average auto at close to one hundred miles per hour in 1927. So he'd be waiting for these deadbeats when they approached the access ramp, and he always collected. His competition had to collect while the towed vehicle was still hooked up, which wasn't too much fun for either tower or towee when dodging upon the drier sand to avoid the waves, logs, rocks and the like, with some distance to get off the beach. This Lozier was always my dad's pride and joy. The motor finally ended up on a loading donkey.

Getting a Tow (Stevens Collection)

Les Ordway and Jack Leavitt

The earliest operations I recall belonged to Les Ordway and Jack Leavitt. Jack's truck was one of a long succession of reworked World War II Army vehicles. Leavitt's rig had the advantage of four-wheel drive, an enclosed cab, and very aggressive tires suited to beach travel. Jack prowled the beach on a regular basis and became our nemesis. In the winter months when prime drift objects floated ashore, he invariably scored the most treasures. We plotted and schemed and vowed vengeance. On several occasions we spotted large Japanese glass fishing floats bobbing in the surf, a highly sought-after item, at the same time he did. We sprinted down from the banks above the beach, foot-racing Jack in his truck. We cursed his advantage and bided our time.

George Malstead and the Texaco Station, from the Late Fifties

Our hero finally arrived in the late 1950s. George Malstead assumed ownership of the old Shell Oil service station on the corner of Hemlock Street and Gower. Burly and solid, George captured our hearts from the outset. A cheerful disposition and proclivity for joshing and joking endeared him to us quickly. He grinned a constant Cheshire cat, jack-o-lantern grin and exuded good fellowship. We nicknamed him "Happy Tooth." George quickly commenced revamping the scruffy old service station to suit his tastes. George was a mean hand with a cutting torch and welding equipment and reveled in automotive creativity. His background included extensive

SHELL OIL COMPANY
CREDIT CARD INVOICE

973744

SOLD TO

CITY & STATE

CARD NO.

LICENSE NO.

THIS COPY CANNOT BE USED FOR TAX REFUND PURPOSES

GEO MALSTEAD 5792
CANNON BEACH ORE 38

DATE 4-15-61

SHELL

SHELL PRODUCTS			QUAN.	PRICE	AMOUNT
GASOLINE	SUPER SHELL	SHELL Gals.			
MOTOR OIL	PREM. X-100 / X-100	GOLDEN SHELL Qts.			
		SALES TAX			
THIS IS A CREDIT SALE NOT A CASH RECEIPT		TOTAL	$		

The charges shown are hereby transferred to SHELL OIL COMPANY. Title to tires, tubes, batteries and accessories is reserved and will not pass to purchaser until full payment is received. Default in any installment payment renders the full balance due.

CUSTOMER'S COPY

The amounts shown include all taxes which the vendor or any prior vendor must pay or is obligated to collect.

RECEIVED BY X

T.B.A. DEFERRED PAYMENT PLAN: ☐ 3 MOS., _____ MOS., ☐ 6 MOS.

Credit card receipt from Malstead's gas station (Grant/Bartl Collection)

work in the shipyards, and considerable automotive painting and custom auto work. He promptly set about retooling an old Dodge Power Wagon of military lineage into a serviceable tow truck. A fierce rivalry developed between George and Jack Leavitt for beach tow clients. Jack's towing business had slumped badly, and we kids saw our chance to wreak revenge. Jack had a scruffy, mean-minded side to him and was reputed to treat his offspring shabbily. We cultivated George and did everything in our power to help his business thrive.

The ancient service station was no small wonder.

"If the termites in this building ever stop holding hands," George would joke, "this building will fall down around us."

We began roaming the beaches seeking tow clients, agents provocateurs on a mission. When we spotted a car stuck and facing imminent destruction from the incoming tide, we sidled up and began our spiel.

"Tide's coming in high today. It looks like you'll need a tow. It's none of my business, really, but I wouldn't call Leavitt. He's shady and real expensive. We can get a tow truck for you. Last week a guy lost his car in the surf right here! Yep, sank out of sight in a crab hole. Lights were still on inside the car. Two feet of seawater over the roof of the car. Totaled. Thing went down like the Titanic! Poor family wet and shivering. Kids crying. Yeah, we'll get our friend George. Hang on! We'll be right back."

George's soft side often put him at cross-purposes in his nascent

*Peter Lindsey's pickup
modified by George Malstead
(Peter Lindsey Collection)*

business venture. A tiny office building stood off the repair bays. A rickety apartment nudged into the air above the service area. Everything swayed and rattled during Sou'westers, singing a sad song of disrepair and vanishing dreams. A well-intentioned proprietor from an earlier day, maybe Old Man Bangs, had applied yellow whitewash to the sere shingles. Now the building appeared to be in the final stages of graying jaundice. In the office, an aged oil stove warmed the interior. A motley of chairs and a couch served the loafers and laggards: "Nothing but a bunch of coastal mutants," someone once commented. Bookkeeping was minimal. I don't remember a cash register, only a "cash drawer."

"How's business going, George?" we would inquire.

George would smile, slide open the cash drawer, and display a few lonely greenbacks and a burgeoning collection of watches, costume jewelry, and trinkets that would make a pawnbroker grimace.

"I yanked a poor young couple out at Hug Point yesterday. Two kids. Hand-me-down clothes. Guy opened up his wallet. Showed me he only had ten bucks. His wife left me that necklace for collateral. 'Pearls,' she told me. Said they'd send me the money as soon as they got home. Pete, it almost broke my heart."

During the off-season, nine months of the year in those times, George began projects. We dug in to help with a vengeance. George concocted a beach buggy scheme. He devised a homegrown engineering design that transmogrified car bodies into truncated pickup trucks. He cut away the back half of a passenger automobile, welded on a petite bed, applied some wooden planks to the refabricated frame, split tire rims, widened the wheels, fused two wheels together for better rear traction, and deflated the tires for better purchase

Aerial photograph, downtown Cannon Beach, 1961 (Grant/Bartl Collection)

in soft sand. Soon a score of serviceable veterans joined the fleet. The bays swelled with a welter of oxidized vehicles, misfit cars of questionable genealogy: Hudson Hornets, Cadillacs, Henry J's, Nash Lafayettes, Fords, Chevs, Studebakers.

Young Men's Pastimes in Cannon Beach in the Sixties

We roamed the beach like Rommel's troops, beachcombing, skylarking, splitting drift logs, locating potential tows. For variety, we jolted along logging roads at speed. Abandoned gravel spur roads overgrown with young alder were sought. The saplings whipped and flayed the car bodies in a manner that pleased us immensely.

Flames and pinstripes dressed up these sand chariots. Every color and tint in the Crayola box appeared. Certain obtuse phrases and slogans individualized the machines. Mine, an old '53 Dodge, had Gothic lettering that said "Cannon Beach Boys" on the cab and a sign warning "Beware! Hongries at Large." Sand and salt played havoc on the chassis and exhaust systems of these rigs. The attrition rate on mufflers was vexing. We discovered that an *Oregon Journal* newspaper box, cylindrical and of the proper diameter, fit very nicely over a failed muffler. Hay-wired onto the manifold pipe, the news box was easily replaced, and the supply, thanks to the Newhouse Publishing Company, apparently endless.

Tommy Stanton's gas station (Grant/Bartl Collection)

Chapter 9

The Texaco Station Changes Hands

Just east of the Shell station, in what is now the public parking lot, stood Van Vleet Logging Company's main garage and corporate offices. Their head mechanic, Tommy Stanton, left the company in the early sixties and purchased the Shell station. Many of us expressed a measure of dismay, even some trepidation. What fate awaited our hangout? The wrench of change troubled us. We heard rumors. The new owner was feisty, apparently, a scrapper. He'd been a flyer during the war, shuttling P-38 fighter planes overseas into Africa and England and had trained pilots at the beginning of the war.

We'd watched the goings on at the truck barn from our vantage point at the station. Friday afternoons the loggers gathered up for a little light celebrating at the garage. Whiskey-generated brouhaha, donnybrooking, cavorting, and mildly bellicose action closed a physically demanding workweek. On the last workday before Christmas, the boss gave each logger a bonus, a fifth of whiskey per man. We young fellows steered well clear of the truck barn on those days. The levity frequently spilled over into the streets surrounding the compound, and we shuddered at the possibilities. Logging was, and continues to be, a rough and tumble business. The men

Loggers in front of the Van Vleet logging office (Amos Collection)

worked and played hard. The Picards, McVeys, Udells, Cantwells, Teubers, Grubmeyers, and the "bull of the woods" Floyd Nelson generated a lot of sparks when they staged a shivaree. We kept a respectful distance.

From Rascals to Lattes

Cannon Beach has become a gentrified and sedate place in the 1990s. The lumpy spots have been effectively ironed out and refined. Young over-amped professionals sip double lattes and dandle laptop computers on their knees. God forbid some whiskey-breath logger, hormones raging, stumbled into them outside a boutique! Our law enforcement people quell such behavior quickly. Subtle filters eliminate the dirt and motes from the civic atmosphere. That was not always the order of things. I remember Saturday night punch-ups at Bill's Tavern, disgruntled patrons pillaging the Sunset Tavern, a rampaging choker setter busting out windows with a chunk of downspout, guns discharged in the middle of Hemlock Street.

Tommy Stanton worked and socialized with that lot, and we weren't sure. All our fears quickly dissolved. Within days we recognized Tommy's unique qualities and all doubts were allayed. Stanton's Shell assumed its own personality.

Sanford and Son would have felt comfortable at Tommy's place. Things began showing up quickly. George operated a somewhat Spartan operation: tools hung on wall silhouettes, tidy concrete under hydraulic jacks, Polish sausages and prawns in gallon jars, job orders filed in a pi-geon-holed desk. Tommy functioned best under adversity and ordered confusion. In the months to come, the most glorious assemblage of odd-ments, tools, and gimcracks filtered through the doorways. I recall beaver pelts curing on a wall, Country Club whiskey in the Bubble Up machine, logging detritus, a junkyard of incongruous body parts and drivetrains, beach drift of every description, tools helter-skelter and harum-scarum. If he had installed a petting zoo, we would have boasted the prototype for *Another Roadside Attraction.*

"Boys," Tommy would say, "I don't mind if you use the tools, but for God's sake don't put them away. I'd never find them."

George had been genteel, benign, methodical. Tommy, lanky, lean, and mildly apoplectic, operated like an eccentric wheel. He began slowly then picked up tremendous speed as he gathered momentum. His motor cranked over at 6,000 rpm when he got under the hood of a car. Sometimes end wrenches and screwdrivers actually flew around the garage. And, boy golly, did the characters ever start showing up!

I have this notion about characters. When this country was young, the spaces were vast. The northern Oregon coast had scant population and limitless nature. Large spaces require powerful spirit and character. The shriveled, pissant existence suburban dwellers accept today would have dumbfounded the people I knew here as a boy. Their personalities colored the community canvas with broad brush strokes and a steady hand. A person might well be a rascal, but he damn well better be a bull-goose rascal, a rascal of proportion and spirit, a rascal among rascals, casting a wide shadow. I watch tourists pull up in their Mercedes-Benz automo-biles, barking and whining like fice dogs, sniping and sniveling. Tommy and his kind would not understand. Their territory was never that small and mean.

Tommy and the Green Stamps

Tommy initiated a policy that virtually guaranteed a coterie of colorful characters hunkered around the office's oil stove. A patron would pull up at the pumps in the late afternoon and fill the tank.

"Do you want Green Stamps, Jim?" Tommy inquired slyly. If the client responded in the affirmative, Tommy invited him inside. He kept the pop machine well stocked with warm Bubble Up soda. A dispenser fastened to the wall held nested twelve-ounce waxed paper cups. Patrons rounded up a chair or a case of motor oil and seated themselves, while Tommy retrieved a fifth of whiskey from a secret place. Tommy circled the room, stewarding the whiskey into client's paper cups, four or five ounces worth chased with a whisper of warm Bubble Up. After five or ten minutes, the wax commenced dissolving inside the cups and tongues began to dance.

Tommy, like all the best people I've ever known, loved a good story. He was a twinkly, blue-eyed, mischievous boy inside a man. I don't think he was Irish, but he should have been. When the poteen started its warm magic under the ribs, the tales began to fly.

Ott Keeps His Eye on the Green Stamps

Ott Cantwell stopped by regularly for Green Stamps after a hard day in the woods. Well, that's not quite correct. He stopped whenever he felt comfortable about his wife, Grace, the "schoolmarm" as he put it, seeing him at the station on her way home from school. Grace drove by in her red '54 Ford Victoria about 5 o'clock, honking in witness of the proceedings. Ott winced and sipped at a quickened pace. Grace would not countenance tipsiness at the supper table.

Ott had a glass eye. Sometimes it would goggle backward in the socket and Ott would stunt around with the thing. In the years I knew him, his appearance reminded me of a lovable chimpanzee, one who has just made off with a bunch of bananas. Ott was a short, stocky, balding gent who spoke in a soft lilting way, as sweet a man as you'd ever meet at a church social. Grace was his match. I don't think God creates their kind anymore. Ott liked a practical joke. His favorite involved the eye.

Some people try to mask their infirmities or physical anomalies. Bald men affect toupees to hide thinning hair. Ladies fill out or diminish body shapes with special undergarments. Not Ott. He did wear glasses, though, and many people simply didn't realize the eye was missing.

Ott held a job as watchman at a timber-loading yard up on Youngs Bay. The job required him to work weekends. A party of friends planned a trip to Astoria during the Scandinavian Festival. They decided to stop by the yard on their way to the celebration and press Ott into coming along for the fun. He listened to their arguments quietly, smiling.

"Well," he said. "I'm responsible for things here and I should stick around. I could get fired if anything went wrong. I've got an idea."

Ott reached up, removed his glasses, and plucked the glass eye out of its socket.

"There," he said, setting the eye firmly on a desk in the office. "Now I can keep an eye on things here while I'm gone!"

The trick I witnessed most often involved the following setup: A bunch of us would be jawing around inside the service station office. A stranger, usually a young person, purchased gasoline and wandered in to square up his bill. Ott would call out to the youngster, and we'd smirk quietly in the corners.

"Boy, my eye is itchin' me somethin' fierce. Must have got something in it. Say, son," he would call out, "hand me that screwdriver over there, would ya?"

The kid would reach over and hand Ott the screwdriver respectfully. At this point, Ott slammed the blade of the screwdriver smartly into the glass orb with several thrusts, clacking and gouging it roughly. We could scarcely contain our mirth, shaking and chortling to ourselves.

"Thanks, son," he'd tell the shocked young man, pulling the thing out of his forehead. "Dang, no wonder that thing itched so bad. See here? It's got mosquito bites all over it!"

I remember one joyous Christmas celebration in the old station particularly vividly. Eino Jakku had brought his old, yellow Cadillac in for muffler repairs. Tommy and the boys had finished up early and were taking their leisure around the oil stove. The Green Stamps flowed freely and jubilation carried the day. Tommy's buddies from Van Vleet's shop sallied across the street and rousted about bringing their bonus whiskey to sweeten the pot. Ott had gotten a jump-start on the rest, and his boots had begun to wobble. Suddenly, we saw Grace drive by in her red Ford.

Honk. Honk. She hit the horn to let us know she knew the score and was headed home.

"Oh, oh," Tommy told Ott. "There's Gracie."

"It's okay. I'll just have one more."

One led to two, and we saw Grace head back north, honking again.

"Oops," said Otto. "Well, I won't be long. Grace is a fine woman. Don't worry. Anyway, it's Christmas."

We engaged in some light badinage regards women and their frailties, their failure to understand the ways of men. Suddenly, Grace materialized as if by magic, laying on the horn in front of the pumps and waving her fist at the office. Ott leapt up like his pants were afire and flailed toward the door. He was invisible for two months.

"Where's Ott Cantwell?" someone would ask.

"He's taken up religion," Tommy told people. "He's in a state of Grace."

Chapter 10
The First Artists Arrive

At some time during the Tommy Stanton era, our first practicing artist, at least the first one during modern times, arrived in Cannon Beach. We knew he was a real artist because he looked unusual, drank wine, and seemed to be inordinately hungry, a real starving artist. One wag of the time said he lived off "the smell of an oily rag."

Frank Lackaff and his friend Ken Grant attended the Commercial Art School in Portland, an institution near the old Bedells store in that city. After graduation, they showed up in these parts. Subsequently, both exerted a significant influence on Cannon Beach and its reputation as an art colony. Frank wore wide-wale cords and saggy sweaters. He smoked an old pipe and had a spritely, boyish grin. He quickly nestled into the community and joined that long roster of characters that gives this place its special appeal.

Frank drove an old 1949 British Anglia, an odd little vehicle, pragmatic and quirky. I think the jet black, little jellybean of a car had spent years of its life in the family's chicken shed in Ridgefield, Washington. Frank became a familiar sight, putting around the village, his auto bristling with an assortment of old easels, burlap bags, pack frames, and sketching supplies in the contraption. Of short stature, Frank seemed somehow European, exotic, free-spirited, novel. In the sometimes stuffy, churchy, working logger town of Cannon Beach, he was something of an anomaly. He painted peculiar portraits on old gunnysacks—they seemed very avant-garde to us. We were only eighteen or nineteen years old. For

M&M building looking east on Second Street, early 1960s (Coaster Construction Collection)

reasons of economy, he hand ground his own paint pigments using a sheet of glass and a muller (he called it a "muler"), blending pigment with linseed oil and beeswax. Heavy-textured creations characterized his early works. The potato sack surfaces absorbed enormous quantities of oil paint.

Frank recalled his arrival in Cannon Beach in the early sixties:

When I drove into town that busy summer of 1962, I needed a place to stay. Somebody steered me to Dick Atherton who had a real estate office on Hemlock Street next to the bakery. Dick had his finger in a lot of pies, property-wise, and one of them was the M&M Building, an asbestos-clad monstrosity at Second and Hemlock, right downtown. He'd taken it over from the estate of the previous owner named Newman who had been murdered in it the year before, or so the story goes. Some fellow who was a little "off" wanted to buy it, and when Newman wouldn't sell, he did him in. I can't remember how he did it, but I think it was something to do with that metal poker at the downstairs fireplace.

The first time I went upstairs in the M&M Building to look over my new home, I was shocked. The whole upstairs, which ran from Hemlock Street almost a whole block back into the marshland by Elk Creek, was unfinished. I felt as if I were stepping into a huge cadaver, the inside of a broken beast. Exposed studs, joists, and rafters, twisted and wracked, were nothing more than the dried and beached bones of a building that was fast being eaten by neglect. Rot and mildew, the gnawing of bug and vermin, and years of abandonment, had left only a shell of what might have been. "Abandon all hope, ye who enter here," I said, jokingly, to my-self, hoping my attempt at humor would perk up my morale.

But it didn't work. And the deeper I got into the M&M Building, the more depressed I became. And when I returned that evening, flashlight and sleeping bag in hand, darkness had added a sinister mood to the building. A man had recently been murdered here. Had they caught the murderer? Was I a little crazy myself in thinking I could get a good night's sleep in a place like this? I beamed the flashlight over my shoulder and then curled into a fetal position in my sleeping bag where I didn't sleep a wink the whole night.

Frank took up quarters in his family's beach cabin on Logan Lane, South Tolovana Park. Situated on a perch in a thicket of shoreside spruce, the little cabin sits above a small swale with a creek emptying onto the beach. To this day, the diminutive building stands immediately above the beach, its rotting shingles and red-trimmed windows catching the brunt of southwest storms, essentially unchanged for half a century. Frank began living and painting there. He'd invite us down for a glass of wine while he painted in the shack, wind rattling the windows, driftwood crackling in the fireplace. Furnishings were sparse: a few metal hospital beds, a spindled chair, an old waffle-iron grill on which he cooked his meals, a few books, some sculptural pieces.

We'd sit and listen to classical and folk music, sip Beaujolais wine, watch Frank sketch the notions for his latest piece. I remember watching a tiny mouse Frank had befriended clambering up and down a brick chimney in the cabin for crumb offerings, Beethoven surging from an old phonograph. The fine smell of mineral spirits hung in the air and fused with that musty beach cabin odor so distinctive and memorable.

The town wasn't always artist friendly, as this incident should serve to illustrate.

One day the county sheriff, Carl Bondietti, stopped me on the street.

"Pete," he leaned out of his prowl car, "I want to talk to you, privately, you understand. This guy Lack-off, I hear he's an artist, a bohemian type. Something of an eccentric. I understand he's a beatnik, beret and so on. Some artists these days belong to the Communist Party. I heard you know him. I just wanted to warn you. I've heard rumors. You know a lot of these artists are dope addicts. Be careful. If you see anything strange, let me know."

I stared at Carl in complete disbelief!

"Carl," I sputtered out, "I have known Frank for a year now. He drinks a glass of wine once in awhile, but that other stuff is ridiculous. Who told you that?"

"People talk," he responded.

As late teens, comments like that just whetted our appetite for rebelliousness. We began wearing old army fatigue jackets and sweatshirts with the sleeves removed, mimicking Maynard G. Krebs, a television character. I remember affecting a pipe and odd sport coats, reading Kerouac and Ferlinghetti. Frank and I became thick friends. He'd let me tag along on painting missions, packing up the old Anglia for jaunts down the beach to paint rocks and seascapes. On particularly splendid spring and fall days, we gathered up picks and shovels and grubbed for the Neahkahnie treasure. Frank's theory, compounded from discussions with old-timers and a "feeling," held that the logical site for the buried treasure was above Falcon Cove, near a small stream. We humped our gear out to the locale, a spot just east of a steep, horseshoe-shaped cliff. We'd root around in salal brush and duff until our energy dissipated, pause long enough for Frank to chew down a headcheese sandwich, and continue our labors. Generally the whole process degenerated into a nap in the sunshine and a lazy daydream.

Art and Towing

After a year or two, Frank developed a reputation as our artist in residence. He succeeded in accumulating a small clutch of paintings and needed a place to showcase his work. Tommy Stanton had a small anteroom appended to the service station office on the south side. Frank located his first gallery in those quarters. He eventually took up residence in the apartment upstairs.

An odd mélange of gas and art patrons filtered through the old building to the mutual benefit of all concerned. Tommy acquired the AAA franchise for the locale. This entailed responding to emergency tow calls at

Frank Lackaff in front of the Sketch Pad Gallery at Stanton's gas station, early 1960s (Lackaff Collection)

unseemly hours of the day. After a period of careful tutelage, Frank gained sufficient prowess to operate the tow truck independently. Tommy gave him free rein to launch the old Dodge Power Wagon on missions of mercy, usually a vehicle fouled in soft sand and teetering on the brink of destruction. As Frank's pard, I often joined him on runs down the beach, the rusty old black beast chuffing and roaring toward a stranded auto, its occupants milling about the vehicle in complete dismay.

Frank never rode easy behind the wheel. The responsibility unhinged him. Late one night a sailor arrived at the station. Frank had invited me over for dinner and a bottle of red wine. We chatted late into the evening and listened to rain whip the thin walls. Loud thumping and hallooing interrupted our conversation.

"Oh, oh," Frank glanced at me, "did you hear that?"

"Yep."

"We'd better go down and have a look."

A sheepish, disheveled young man hailed us from the street. The wonky gig lines on his navy uniform would have confined him to quarters for a month.

"We're on our honeymoon," he explained, "our car's stuck on the beach and the ocean's around the wheels. I don't have much money."

"We'll fire up the truck. Hop in and we'll go have a look."

Frank and I walked around to the tow truck. Wind-driven rain careened around the building, force 10 on the Beaufort scale. The sailor lurched into the cab of the truck and fished a bottle of whiskey out of his coat.

"We've been celebrating!"

"Congratulations," Frank said.

We thumped off Ecola Ramp onto the spare beach, surf licking at the tires. When we arrived at the old Ford, a young woman oozed out of the car, confused and bleary. Her new husband went to the car and got inside. Frank backed the truck toward the vehicle. We maintained a prudent interval between the car and our truck. I leapt out and fastened a cable to the Ford's frame.

"Keep the wheels straight," I shouted over the wind. "Put the gearshift into neutral, and we'll tow you back to the ramp."

I ran back to the truck cab, soaking wet, and jumped inside. The wind spat a sugaring of sand on the windshield. The car behind us was barely discernible in the blackness.

"Well, here goes nothing," Frank said to me chuckling. "I think this lever here should haul in the cable."

We sat in the cab listening to the grind of the winch. Suddenly, I saw lights in the air behind us.

"Stop! Stop!" I yelled at Frank. We had yanked the car completely off the ground. The Ford was airborne and dangling from the tow truck gantry. Frank and I dashed frantically back to the couple.

"Are you all right?"

The young marrieds were embracing in the front seat, apparently oblivious.

"Oh yeah. We're fine. We're in love!"

As we drove back to the station, Frank looked over at me and commented, "You sure see all kinds, don't you."

Chapter 11

Coming of Age in Cannon Beach

A Logger Talks to God

Once, in a time now long gone, a small, weathered tavern sat on the west side of Hemlock Street, north of Second Street. The proprietor was a curmudgeonly old Polish stump of a man named Stanley Wytaski. His frugality attained legendary status in our little town.

On my twenty-first birthday, Tommy Stanton took me out on the town with my friend Frank Lackaff to celebrate with my first legally purchased beer. He insisted we go to Stanley's Sunset Tavern and make Stanley buy me a beer on the house. Tommy told the following story as we sat at the Sunset's bar on that occasion. Stanley listened sullenly behind the bar:

One day a logger was working up behind Cannon Beach setting chokers and complaining. Suddenly, a ferocious voice came out of the sky, asking what all the griping was about. The logger looked up and realized it was God talking, so he started to explain what a miserable life he had been leading. His only hope was that he might go to "a better place of rest" when he died.

God looked down and said, "Well, I'll tell you what I'll do. If you can accomplish a few things that need doing around here—projects that I haven't had time for—I'll make sure you get into Heaven." The logger agreed.

God said, "The first thing I want you to do is move that big mountain off there, Saddle Mountain, farther south, closer to Cannon Beach." So the logger worked for years and finally finished moving it a shovelful at a time. Then he called to God, and God spoke to him and said, "That's good, but I need the North Fork of Elk Creek moved about two miles farther west." So the logger slaved away for years and finally rerouted the creek and went to call on God again. God said, "That's good, but there's one more thing you've got to do, and then you can be assured of a place in Heaven."

"What's that?" asked the logger. "Go down to Stanley's Sunset Tavern in Cannon Beach," said God, "and sit there drinkin' 'til he buys you a beer on the house. When he does that, you can be sure of a place in Heaven." As the story goes, you can go down to that tavern to this very day, and that logger is still sitting there waitin' for a free beer.

After Tommy finished the story, Stanley nodded over to us and said, "What do you boys want? It's on the house."

Chapter 12

More Characters

I guess every small town has its characters, but Cannon Beach has been blessed with a particularly rich vein, a mother lode, that I would pit against any place its size. Some had surnames, patronyms, Christian names, others just nicknames by which we identified them.

Old "Preach" cohabited with a string of recently bereaved widows. He specialized in elderly ladies whose husbands had passed to the Great Beyond, sympathizing with them and sharing their inheritance. The community sniggered, but I never recall any complaints from the widows. He lived in an old gray '49 Nash. The back seat folded down into a bed, a selling point in those days. He stayed in the car between trysts.

A toothless ex-convict who called himself "Beargrease" showed up in the mid-fifties. Beargrease affected a swept-wing hairdo, highway patrol glasses, engineer boots, and a scurvy T-shirt. He looked like Jack Nicholson whirled around for several revolutions in a cement mixer. He grinned in an unsettling fashion, "like a possum eating poop," as one local put it. Beargrease took a fancy to the Conservative Baptist minister's fourteen-year-old daughter and staged an abortive elopement. I suspect the scandal prompted a fit of praying for his immortal soul.

An obese, stubble-jowled man named Bob Smith lived in a cabin on the Canadian side of Elk Creek. Smith helped caretake Ecola Park. He picked his teeth venomously and ate prodigiously. He drove a black '48 Ford pickup. Bob weighed about four hundred pounds. When he drove through town, his sheer mass caused the truck to list severely to the left.

Evie Boothby, standing in the back of the boat, at the Round Table restaurant, flood of 1967 (Marie Marshall, postmistress, and Phyllis Richetts in prow of boat) (Grant/Bartl Collection)

During slack time, Bob would do stunts. If he got a crowd of young people around, he would take a bow and broad-point hunting arrows, shoot the arrows straight up in the sky, and then sag his huge girth onto the ground. He lay there, a huge mountain, spread-eagled, as the arrows pierced the earth. This primitive game of Russian roulette never failed to please.

The Dog Lady, a spinster, lived on Hemlock Street at Jefferson Street. The Dog Lady took in orphaned animals, strays, crumpled birds. Unfortunately, she wasn't beyond kidnapping an occasional local pet. Jingles, the Sroufe family pet, a mongrel with wanderlust, drifted off for a week and was struck by a car. While his broken jaw healed, the Dog Lady fed him broth through a soda straw placed between his teeth.

We had a bachelor, Mr. Mullins, "Moon," living in a shack next to the skating rink. Shelby McGinnis, another aging bachelor, lived in a set of abandoned railroad cars just south of the Warren Hotel. Shelby decorated his yard with porcelain sculpture—several dozen close-stools, white commodes glistening alabaster in the sun. Today, the code enforcement officer would visit Shelby and confront him. In those past days, yard art was commonplace.

We had a whole tribe of Boothbys. The young Boothbys apparently began smoking Camel straights at birth. For many years the family operated the Round Table Restaurant, famed for its enormous round table, a center for local gossip and discussions.

A man we all called "Honey Pot" wove shingles at the Arch Cape Shingle Mill. The words "Honey Pot" were painted on the door of his '48 Plymouth coupe. An old photo in Bill's Tavern shows the car parked in front of Bill's in the fifties. That's where it stood most afternoons at six o'clock. Mr. Honey Pot, a stocky little man with a paintbrush moustache, enjoyed several pints of ale after a day of shingle weaving. Every evening, without fail, he would stagger out into the street, search up and down Hemlock, and ask the world at large, "Where's my car? Someone's taken my car!" We would laugh and nudge one another. In the 1950s, only five or six cars would be parked on Hemlock at dusk. The Plymouth usually sat no farther than fifty feet from the tavern door.

Chapter 13

Kidding Around In the Fifties

The Waves Roller Rink and Its Cast

The Waves Roller Rink had its cast of characters: dear Mrs. Walker who ran the sweet shop, and the Schade family—managers of the rink—including their daughter, Georgina, a ringleted blond who throbbed most of the young male hearts in town. We young fellows often kidded one another about our erotic dreams.

"I had a dream about Georgina last night."

"Oh yeah? So did I."

"Hey, now, she was in my dream. You leave her alone."

Some towns are one-horse, others, well. . . .

Georgina skated into our adolescent hearts. As a scratchy old recording of the "Beer-Barrel Polka" or "There's a Tavern in the Town" filled the hall, Georgina glided effortlessly around the maple floor, her yellow hair serpentining past, her doe eyes taking the measure of the worshippers.

On weekends, a quiet logger man showed up at the Waves Rink. He was a regular fixture, tall and slender, carefully groomed, balding, solitary. He set the standard for roller skating to which we all aspired. I never knew his name. We simply called him Mr. Backwards. Upon arrival, he carefully unpacked his personal set of skates, slipped them on, and flowed around the rink like greased honey. He moved like wind-blown silk, effortlessly spinning from normal forward motion to a posture that glided his body backwards around the floor. He had an uncanny sense for objects impeding his progress as he spun and twirled—a stumbling child, a couple

Street Scene - Cannon Beach - Oregon   5-42-B smith

Lawson's Drugs (Lent Collection)

skating together. As he skated, he whistled softly, keeping his hands in his pockets, a dream of motion. Occasionally, he skated with Georgina or her mother, the only suitable partners for a man who had attained such prowess. We tried to emulate his moves with scant success. Maybe someday, if we got good enough, Georgina would skate with one of us!

The Bowling Alley

The bowling alley sat across the street, solitary, on poles above the wetland. In my day, the alley was a summer thing. Many young people hired on as pinsetters, a first summer job, earning five cents a line for hand setting small duck pins. One threw small balls, about the size of those used for bowling on the green. Easily hefted, the small balls allowed for serious abuse of bowling decorum. The young pinsetters made fine targets, leaping hastily above the floor to avoid a cannon ball winged at their legs. The proprietor kept a wary eye for delinquency and youthful swagger.

The Drug Store Stories

When I was a kid, Cannon Beach had two drug stores, Lawson's and Newman's Original Drug Store. Lawson's Drugs sat just north of Second

Newman's Drug Store (Coaster Construction Collection)

Street on the west side of Hemlock, a tiny, false-front building, low and squatty. Most days, Mr. Lawson stood outdoors greeting passersby, an elderly, florid gentleman, dressed in a dark conservative suit, his white hair neatly sheared in a short cut, chewing on an unlit Cuban cigar. The cigar rarely left his mouth and was never ignited.

Newman's Original Drug Store occupied the southeast corner of Second Street and Hemlock, site of the current M&M Building. I knew Don Newman as an irascible old egret, stalking around the cavernous building, pecking at merchandise and muttering. The Hemlock Street portion of the building housed the store. Several thousand square feet of unfinished space made up the balance. Don had a soda fountain counter and an enormous fireplace, a Bartels construct, on the east wall of the store. Most of the store housed what were once described as "notions." Don occupied a peculiar merchandising niche, providing aisle upon aisle of kites, sand buckets, trinkets, souvenirs, penny candy, post cards, and unmentionable plastic objects. At the time I knew him, he had befriended a somewhat stolid live-in mistress. She poured us real fountain Cokes and operated the cotton candy machine. Don had a fine stock of patent medicines and boxes filled to bursting with mail-order eyeglasses. One simply sorted through the boxes and tried on a pair until a suitable fit and magnification resulted.

I think Don viewed us as a necessary nuisance, a nickel here and a dime there. Toward closing time, he usually stoked up a roaring fire in the fireplace and commenced sipping whiskey at the fountain counter. At this hour of the day, he became very voluble and talkative, capable of long flights of testy diatribe. We went in mornings and afternoons. Don didn't like things that upset his daily round. Naturally, some young scamps enjoyed raising his ire.

Don had an abiding fear of young scalawags making off with his merchandise. He hovered and fidgeted about the huge store, fretful and wary. We would mosey about nonchalantly, lifting and poking at things, spreading ourselves out for best effect.

"Hey, you kids either buy something or get out of here!" he would fume at us. I'm certain his pulse rate doubled when we sauntered in from the street.

Our favorite trick was to send one kid in to try to purchase condoms. In those unenlightened times, young people were not appropriate condom customers. We knew Don dreaded our cheekiness.

The kid selected ambled up to the counter shyly and made this request: "I'd like to buy some fish skins."

"Dammit, I've told you before I won't have it. You're too young. What are you going to do with them, anyway? You wouldn't know what to do with them. What's wrong with you kids today? Your morals are disgusting."

"Well, they're for my cat."

Leonard Gerritse Jr. speaks of Don in his journal:

He was a confirmed bachelor, and his store was pretty much always a one-man operation. So when he would break for lunch, he would usually prepare himself something to eat, and sit down at the full-length counter down one side of the building. Doors in front were full width, accordion-type, and the pits to open or close, so he would put a sign alongside where he was eating saying "out to lunch." Then if someone came in and inquired about anything, he would simply point to the sign and go on eating.

You had to have good intestinal fortitude to order anything other than packaged food or drink. Don had a huge English bulldog, ferocious look-

ing but a real pussycat, named Bud. Bud had an ongoing sore on top of his tail, where it was attached and in plain sight of all onlookers. Don had a small bottle of Bismuth Violet he applied to this spot with an old tooth-brush he kept in the bottle. Now, if you came in while he was painting his dog's tail, he would put this toothbrush back in the bottle, pick up a bar towel that had had considerable mileage from the washing machine, wipe his hands perfunctorily, and ask how he could serve you at the foun-tain! It took a strong stomach to even remember what you wanted! We usually ended up with a Nesbitt's orange or mint-flavored drink, as this required a minimum of handling.

Chapter 14
Town Commerce—Mostly Sroufe

A surprising congress of grocery and mercantile stores rose and fell in Cannon Beach in its early years: the Wave Crest Store, Craigies Store, the Tolovana Store, Sage's, Lanphere/Spaulding's Store, Price's Campground, Smith's Store and Fish Market on Tanana and Hemlock. In my day, Nichols's Grocery sat on the east side of Hemlock at Van Buren, Sage's gas station and store operated on the corner next to the lumberyard, the Campground store remained on Elk Creek, Woodward's Grocery stood across the street from Kruschke's Candy Kitchen, the Tolovana Store and Locke's Grocery and Post Office served Tolovana Park, and Sroufe's Grocery stood smack in the heart of downtown Cannon Beach.

J. Harley and Margaret Sroufe owned and operated their store in the 1950s and '60s. Well-seasoned, the building had been in operation since the turn of the century. The original grocery building now contains Osburn's Ice Creamery. My first job at fourteen was stock boy at the store, thirteen dollars a month, working weekends and after school. My duties included hand marking prices on canned goods with felt pen, dressing vegetables, stocking shelves, carrying groceries, sweeping the front deck and sidewalk.

Harley Sroufe in front of Sroufe's Grocery (Sroufe Family Collection)

Left to right: an unidentified gentleman, Harley and Margaret Sroufe, street side at Sroufe's Grocery (Sroufe Family Collection)

The Sroufes kept a finger on the community pulse. Harley gathered snippets of gossip and goings-on and relayed information to his customers. When summer families arrived, Harley logged their return in his memory bank. An amazing repository of information, he could tell you if the Williamsons were down, what time the tide was low, if the huckleberries had ripened, what children had been hired as guides at the stables.

By informal agreement, each merchant policed and swept the street and sidewalk adjacent to his business. On warm dog day mornings in the summers of my youth, it frequently fell on me to sweep the sidewalk and gutter. On fine August mornings, a sweet stillness held time suspended in a dream. The old store had two enormous windows facing the street. A system of ropes and pulleys allowed these hinged windows to be opened and elevated, completely removing any barriers between the sidewalk and the store's interior. During the summer months, those windows remained opened during business hours. We rolled or carted stands of fresh produce to the wide wooden porch facing the street. Lazily working the broom along the concrete, the smell of fresh strawberries, Crenshaw melons, and peaches hung in the salt air. On very quiet mornings, a person could hear the ice machine humming in its building clear at the other end of town. The hypnotic swishing of the broom bristles, the muted store sounds, the soft mewing of gulls offshore, all drew me toward languor

Harley and Margaret Sroufe (Sroufe Family Collection)

and reverie. Perhaps Mr. Sroufe would save me from falling asleep at my broom handle.

"Peter, we just got a new wheel of well-aged Tillamook cheddar. Here, I just cut some off. Try a piece."

Harley was a kind and generous man. With three sons, he had a decent notion about what kept boys ticking. He'd sometimes let me tag along on personal deliveries to special customers. Much beloved by the permanent citizenry and summer people alike, Harley lingered and chatted with people in their homes as we made the rounds. He beachcombed passionately. One of his pet delivery/beachcombing vehicles, a 1948 Chevrolet panel truck, had been swapped for a bottle of whiskey.

Chapter 15
The Great Fish Float Hunts

Leon Settum and Harley shared honors as "King of the Japanese Fish Floats." Leon's cabin nestled in, hugging the clay banks south of Silver Point. For decades, Leon worked his stretch of beach, combing the special places where tidal eddies deposited drift. His collection of hand-blown Japanese glass floats was legendary. A small stream cut through blue clay and vegetation adjacent to his house. Contained within the banks of the stream, clusters of glinting, green orbs shimmered in profusion. Thousands of green and blue-green glass fishing floats, many several feet in circumference, filled the streambed. The floats resembled an enormous clutch of gargantuan frog eggs. The Silver Point Slide of the early 1970s sluiced this magnificent trove of Japanese glass into the sea.

I've never been much on "thingness"; stuff seems to collect around most Americans like dung beetles. I must confess, though, that the highly prized glass floats infected my family in queer ways. During our first winter, particularly fierce storms deposited a rich horde of floats. Harley Sroufe harvested mercilessly, working up and down the tide line like a farmer bringing in a winter crop. He let me ride in the old panel truck, in company with his sons, and taught me the lore and signs.

"We need to get down just after high tide. Strong west winds, due west and blowing steadily—they're the best. When the *velella* show up [*Velella velella* is a small blue jelly fish related to the Portuguese man-of-war], that's a really good sign. Fishing floats come in when the *velella* get blown onto the beach. I usually find them concentrated pretty much in

Glass floats from one storm (Scott Rekate Collection)

the same places time after time, around Haystack Rock, near the mouth of Elk Creek, at the base of Chapman Point."

Harley taught us well. That winter we ranged the beach feverishly, obsessively, impassioned by the strange lure of things round, green, transparent. My sleeping hours were fraught with float dreams. Our current ace beachcomber, Steve McLeod, claims this is common to badly addled combers. In my dreams, I walked a solitary stretch of beach, green glass balls shimmering everywhere, emerald spheres of glass carpeting the edge of the sea. In these troubled flights of fancy, I ran pell-mell down the beach gathering balls frantically in an enormous gunnysack. I awoke anxious and troubled by my greed.

Harsh conditions prevailed. We bundled in rain gear and sou'westers. If high tide occurred at night, we visited the beach and worked the drift line, regardless of the hour. Coleman lanterns and powerful flashlights illuminated the track. First light brought the most rewards. Before day broke, we trudged sleepily to a favorite spot. When fresh footprints appeared along our line of travel, our hearts sank.

"Damn, someone beat us to it!"

"Probably old man Banks."

"Don't be so pessimistic. It was probably just a lady walking her dog."

"Yeah, sure, fat chance. That big old boot print sure looks like a lady's."

During those years, the Lindseys entered the madness with great gusto. We tramped the beach like Sherman's Army, hauling the spoils home and gloating over our finds. Crab floats festooned the trees in the yard and dangled obscenely over our rail fence. Green floats lined windowsills and mantel. Curious debris and oddments collected: a weather buoy, a ceramic Korean burial urn, saké bottles, hatch covers, salmon plugs, Gordian knots of hemp rope, bottles with messages inside, wooden fish boxes, gaff hooks, naval canisters, crab pots.

We were in trouble.

When the two-by-four rafters in our garage began sagging under the sheer mass of scavenged wood, we knew it was time to cease and desist. We discovered powderpost beetles chewing on mahogany planks collected from the beach. They commenced to jump ship and began nibbling at structural members.

I still remember those days, though, with a measure of sentiment. My Scottish side delighted in getting something free. The thrill of the hunt quickened one's pulse. Each cycle of winter tides delivered new wonders, curiosities borne on the Kuroshio Current from lands distant and exotic.

Chapter 16
The Olson Boys

I think it's about time to account for the Olson boys: Vic, Bud, and their dad, Olie. When I think of Vic, a smile always creases my face. The Olson story goes something like this:

Gerry Sroufe and I lounged on a small bench just north of the roller rink. The day was fresh, peaceful, delicate with the soft quality of early spring. A sudden roar-up at the north end of town seized our attention. A huge motorcycle slammed down main street and jarred to a stop in front of us. Its rider reared back on the seat and dismounted. He wore full leathers, reflective sunglasses, a cap styled after SS storm troopers, engineer boots, and a foot-long key chain. The man behind the glasses had dense red sideburns and a smouldering Pall Mall straight in his yellowed lips. He removed the cigarette from his lips and rolled his tongue around his mouth. When he began to speak, we noticed he only had a few teeth.

"You from around here, boys?" he asked us.

"Yeah."

"Keep an eye on this bike for me," he directed us. "But be careful. She's a killer. Two men died on this Harley. She's mean. Nothing like my brother Bud's bike, though. Eleven men died on that machine. Whew! The Devil himself couldn't ride 'er. Bud'll be here any time. He just got out of prison for impersonatin' an officer. Stoppin' people up there on the beach up at Gearhart. Just like the highway patrol."

Sure enough. A few minutes later brother Bud wheeled in, nodded toward us with a shifty grin, kicked the stand under his bike, and sauntered down the street.

"Bud don't say much," the man told us. "My name's Vic. The Olsons will be living here now. You'll be hearing about us."

The man called Vic attempted to jumpstart the killer bike several times to no avail, leapt off the thing and began abusing it. After a few perfunctory kicks at the tire, he remounted. The thing fired up in a cloud of smoke and blasted down the street.

"Yahoo!" he yelled as he roared out of sight.

"What do you make of that?" Gerry asked me. We could only shrug and shake our heads.

With the arrival of Vic Olson, we had our very own Baron Munchausen. Vic would have been elected president of the Burlington Liars' Club hands down. In short order we even coined our own term, "Vicin'." If a person stretched the truth a little bit, someone would say, "You ain't Vicin' me, are ya?"

We had a secret place where we older boys gathered to swap stories, smoke secretly, maybe drink some homemade beer or jugs of Silver Spur wine lifted from a parent's private stash. We called the place "The Hole," a cleared spot in a thicket of trees and blackberry vines off behind the Waves Roller Rink. Vic held court there, regaling us with stories about his airplanes, the Korean War, fishing and hunting:

I remember that time I was in the Korean War. Infantry. I was guardin' the perimeter. One night, I saw movement outside. White shapes in the snow. A North Korean regiment was preparin' to attack. I charged them, throwin' grenades and firing. A machine gun opened up on me, but I kept on. I eliminated 'em and staggered back to the camp. When I got back, the sarge yelled at me, "Olson! My God, man, look at you! Your guts are hangin' out." I looked down and realized my whole intestines were outside my belly I'd been shot up so bad. They patched me up. Put plastic intestines in me. I've got silver plates all over my body. Here. [He would grab one of our hands and place it on his balding head]. Feel that plate in there? That's pure silver. My lungs are all plastic too. That's why I can hold this smoke in my lungs so long.

At this point he would demonstrate by taking an enormous puff of cigarette smoke and holding it in his lungs.

Vic had done it all. He told us about the twenty-four-cylinder Duesenberg he owned up in Goldendale, Washington. That mythical power-plant reposed in a chicken coop there, waiting for future deliverance, "if the damn chicken crap hasn't ruined it." Vic claimed he had a private airplane with guns mounted on the wings. The guns fired shotgun shells. He once shot a whole flock of geese with that aircraft, the gun barrels glowing beet red and melting.

Vic did security work and a stint as park ranger at Ecola Park. He was a canny fisherman. No one challenged that fact. He claimed he could read a fish's thoughts. I fully believe he could. I think I've seen the evidence. Vic had a truly inventive imagination, keen on taking a novel situation or the facts at hand and weaving them into a fine tale, albeit tall at times. I think this tale, collected, archived, and published in several folklore anthologies serves to illustrate that skill.

Chapter 17
Rock Fishing Below Ecola Point

On choice spring days, we'd gather up for a rock fishing expedition at Haystack, Silver Point, or the rock outcroppings below Ecola Point. We targeted rockfish, greenling, cabezon, surf perch, and Irish lords. We generally hauled out a few six-foot crowbars and a tire iron or two to remove mussels from the rocks. We prized huge rocks from the sandy tide pools and scoured around in the broken shell stock for butter clams and cockles. Sometimes we brought a sledgehammer with us. When we found likely looking sandstone boulders filled with holes, we bashed the rocks to pieces and extracted piddocks, or rock oysters, from their hiding places inside the rocks. This practice, in hindsight, was not particularly sound from an environmental standpoint. Nor was our application of Clorox to splash-zone boulders as a means of harvesting kelp worms for bait. I apologize. We just didn't know any better.

On this fine day, Frank Lackaff, Vic, a few locals, and my girlfriend Pamela scrambled out to the South Needle. We had all the artillery. We'd stopped at Mac McCoy's Service Station or Tommy's Shell for a sack full of old rusty spark plugs. The plugs made fine sinkers, cheap and expendable. Lead sinkers cost too much, and the rate of loss on sinkers was wondrous. The best fishing for rock species was in crannies at the toe of huge boulders. Hangups plagued our fishing. Each surge of seawater drove sinker and hook into a crevice or cluster of mussels, virtually guaranteeing a snagged line.

Pamela wore tennis shoes, a cotton blouse, and pants that were called pedal pushers. This was her first rock fishing adventure. Vic pulled out a

Ecola Point in distance (Lent Collection)

sheath knife and commenced clobbering clusters of mussels off the rocks. He launched into a protracted dissertation, recalling past fishing expeditions, the pratfalls of surf fishing, lore, and expertise. The time-proven bait for surf fishing was mussel flesh. Prying open the shells, Vic deftly stripped the serrated orange flesh from the edge of the mussel shell. As he removed the meat, he carefully slipped his index finger inside the soft tissue to search for pearls. Mussels often create small irregular shaped pearls around intrusive material. On this day he located a particularly large pearl and proffered it to Pamela. She had no pockets in her pedal pushers to carry the prize and decided to place it in her mouth for safekeeping. That prompted this story from Vic:

I remember a time a couple of years ago when I was fishing down by Pacific City. A bunch of fellows and I were fishing then, just like we are here today, and I was slicing open mussels for bait. I found a few big pearls. A gal came along and wanted a pearl to take home for jewelry, so I gave it to her. She had no pockets in her pedal pushers, just like you don't, so she stuck the pearl in her mouth so she wouldn't lose it as she walked from the slippery rocks to the beach. About half way off the rocks, she slipped and swallowed the damn thing. She was real sorry to lose it like that, but figured it wouldn't hurt her any, and she could just crap it out of her system.

Well, about five months later her belly began to ache and swell up. Her family figured she had gotten knocked up by some fellow, but they wouldn't take her to a doctor because they were ashamed of the whole damn business. They sent her off to a home to live while she had the baby. Well, about two months later the poor girl died. When they took an autopsy on her and cut her belly open, they found a half-grown octopus inside! That girl hadn't swallowed a pearl from a mussel at all, she'd swallowed a damn octopus egg.

Vic had a vivid imagination.

He had a flair for crafting a riveting tale from whatever materials he had at hand. I recall a summer's morning in August. Extreme heat had created dense inversion fog along the shoreline. Several of us had gathered at a beach cabin to apply cedar shingles on a drooping roof. Vic showed up and commenced wooling us:

Well, boys, I see yer going to go at that roof today. I don't know as how that's such a good idea. Let me tell you somethin' that happened to me one time. I was helpin' another feller up on Clatsop Plains shingle an old barn. We come out one mornin' to begin and, by God, if that thick pea-soup fog hadn't settled in over everything. Couldn't see your nose in front of your face. Well, we cussed it, but figgered we better get the job done, so we climbed up on the roof and started makin' the shinglin' hatchets fly. We were goin' great guns. Layed down three square by mid-mornin'.

Well, about that time, the sun begun to break through. Started to burn off that fog real quick. The other feller went over to the edge of the roof to look at somethin'. All of a sudden that whole end of the roof caved in! That poor bastard fell plumb down to the ground, roof and all. Rode the whole damn thing down to the ground.! Unbeknownst to us, we'd shingled way out over the edge of that building. The fog was so Goddam thick, it held

those shingles up in the air! When the fog cleared, it just flat caved in. You
boys be careful up there now, you hear?"

Vic possessed a motley of old firearms. He generally had substantial blocks of nonemployed time, time for fishing, yarning, and hunting. He'd take us boys on long hunting capers in the foothills behind Cannon Beach, gypsying around Sugarloaf Mountain, Onion Peak, and the Tolovana Mainline Road. We savaged old stumps, tin cans, distant targets with a rude collection of Enfield rifles, Winchester carbines, .22s, and shotguns. We stalked, read sign, slipped furtively through alder thickets, listened for the whistle of bull elk carried on the wind. Mostly, we swapped stories and laughed at Vic's tales and bawdy songs.

Here's one he told us, a variant of a Munchausen tale, if I'm not mistaken:

This here feller went out hunting, and he drove up into the country. And he seen this deer walkin' along, and he got out his big old powerful magnum rifle. He watched this deer for a little while, and about the time he got his sights set on it, the deer jumped behind this big tree.

That made him madder than the dickens, so he whirled around with his rifle and shot the other way! Shot it behind him! And it was the last day of huntin' season, so he just emptied his rifle out, got back in his car, and drove home.

So, next huntin' season opened up, why, he went back up to this same spot. Here comes a deer walking up there, and he loaded his rifle right quick, and he pointed it, and he went to pull the trigger. Just about the time he went to pull the trigger, the darn deer jumped behind a tree! So he pulls his rifle back and all at once the deer jumps straight in the air and dropped over dead.

"So he walked around behind the deer and looked at it. And that bullet that he'd fired the year before had went around the world and come back and smacked that deer dead center."

Chapter 18

The Cannon Beach Water and Sewer System,
Such as They Were

Lee Firebaugh owned and operated the Cannon Beach water system at the time my family moved to Cannon Beach. The city purchased the existing system following incorporation. Much of the piping had been in place for decades, fallible arteries and capillaries of cast iron and wood, drawing water from a lovely artesian spring. The spring water source and catch basin sat in a grand stand of ancient cedars several miles up the Warren Road.

The water works were a seat-of-the-pants, Band-Aid proposition. Lee, an elderly and dear little dumpling of a man, and Olie, Vic Olson's dad, performed maintenance. Olie had prominent, bushy, red sideburns and a slow honey drawl. He looked like a character actor portraying a moonshiner. The two of them spent a good deal of time pottering about in ditches and driving through town in an old bright red Jeep converted into an oddly truncated panel truck.

One day the two of them were excavating a septic tank at the presbytery, home of the newly arrived Presbyterian minister, a pious young man by all accounts, recently wedded. Something had been clogging the septic tank piping. Water had been backing up in the shower and kitchen sink, a nuisance for the young couple engaged in God's work and unsightly as well. Olie and Lee began digging up the septic tank to assay the situation.

I happened to wander by on East Washington Street just as they finished shoveling the last dirt from the lid of the rusted iron tank. After a

PURE-BUT-NOT-PURIFIED

OUR SOURCE IS AT THE SPRING

CANNON BEACH WATER CO., INC., CANNON BEACH, OREGON

Cannon Beach Water System letterhead (Grant/Bartl Collection)

mild struggle, the lid was removed and the contents exposed to the light of day. A generous sea of latex condoms filled the tank to the brim and choked off the influent piping. The two gazed at the scene, leaning on their shovels.

"My, my, my!" Olie offered, nudging the earthen spoils with his boot.

Lee, a pillar of the church, stared at the contents, smiled like a gar, and offered up his comment. "I would say our new minister is a very active man!"

L. David (Dave) Firebaugh took over the water business from his father. Dave, a large, blustering character, changed the operation and modernized the system.

He began installing water meters on select buildings suspected of heavy water use. One of the first to get a meter was Tommy Stanton's Shell station. Dave showed up one morning during Tommy's absence. Tommy had taken vacation for a few weeks, and Frank Lackaff looked after things in his stead. Dave and his helper guffawed around by the street corner for a while and started digging.

"What's going on, Dave?" someone asked.

"Aww, we're putting in a meter here. Tommy uses a lot of water, we've noticed. Times are changing. He may just have to pay a little more, that's all."

"Maybe you ought to wait 'til he gets back."

"Nah, we need to get this done."

A week later, Tommy returned from vacation. He noticed the new meter right off. Now, Tommy was one of the sweetest men ever to drive down Hemlock Street, but he had a very low flashpoint. Tommy's face reddened up like a raw pot roast.

"That dirty son of a bitch!" he said. "If he thinks he's going to put one over on me, he's got another thing comin'. Watch the pumps for me, boys, I'll be right back."

Tommy returned a few minutes later with two sacks of concrete. He immediately mixed up a batch of concrete, lifted the meter lid, and filled in the meter cavity to the brim. He mushed the lid into the wet concrete and dusted off his hands.

"That should settle the problem."

When Dave showed up a few days later, a major confrontation occurred. The two men squared off in the street and began jostling and pushing one another, Tommy jabbing big old Dave in the chest with his finger. I will not quote the unseemly verbal exchange in deference to lady readers. As I recollect, the concrete-filled meter remained until the station burned to the ground several years later.

Chapter 19
Finding and Burning Wood for Warmth

Wood played an important part in early village life. A few families had oil or electric forced-air furnaces by the fifties, but most relied on fireplaces and wood stoves for heat. The cutting, splitting, hauling, and stacking of endless cords of firewood filled the hours of our lives. Our family heated its home exclusively with wood until the late 1970s. Fortuitously, wood was plentiful and easily accessed. Every winter a fine crop of logs drifted onto the beach, a veritable sampler of fine timber, domestic and foreign: Douglas fir, spruce, hemlock, Philippine mahogany, oak, alder, red cedar, Port Orford cedar, redwood, mountain ash, vine maple. We became swift adepts, savvy in log selection and identification. A discerning eye quickly culled out less desirable logs, "piss fir," punky wood, treated pilings. In questionable cases, a blaze with an axe or a quick saw kerf settled the issue. A log battered and bruised in ocean passage could be sampled with a few swift slices and then split to reveal interior grain and texture. A few sniffs from a talented nose revealed special qualities. I vividly recall the rich, musky incense emanating from a grand log of Port Orford cedar, a regal timber, rare and treasured. Alaskan yellow cedar, wind shunted from the currents of the great North Pacific Gyre, had its own odor, medicinal and pungent.

We harvested "lily pads" joyfully, huge round slabs of timber presliced and darn easy pickins. A few desultory whacks with an axe pared the pad into lovely stove wood, simple as slicing a soft cheese.

My brother Tim Lindsey reminded me of a rich time for beach woodcutters, circa 1963–64. Several wave-driven log injuries prompted

Harvey Lindsey (extreme right) chatting with beach visitors, 1970 (Lindsey Collection)

Governor Hatfield to issue a memo to the Oregon Highway Department. Large logs had struck bystanders on ocean beaches. Perhaps something could be done. The Highway Department, in its infinite wisdom, decided to initiate a program aimed at minimizing log danger on Oregon beaches. The department sent workers who chain-sawed potential offenders into four- to five-foot lengths!

We gleefully slung the pre-cut logs into our pickup beds and hauled them home, a painless and laborsaving caper. A five-foot stick fit handsomely in our enormous Bartels fireplace. Life was sweet! Bless the government.

During the 1960s and 1970s, countless two-by-two mahogany boards drifted onto the beach. I think they may have served as stickers for deck loads of stacked lumber aboard timber vessels. My father, Harvey, accumulated thousands of these small boards and gained some notoriety in the community. He was a familiar figure on the beach, an elderly gentleman in a Scottish tam-o'-shanter, an ample head of snow-white hair and full beard, walking his twice-daily rounds to Silver Point, collecting and

Arch Cape shingle mill, early 1960s (Noonan/Schiffman Collection)

chatting with other walkers. People began calling them "Harvey sticks" and saved them for his wood stash.

My first vehicle, deemed acceptable and reasonably safe for an adolescent with foolhardy proclivities, was a 1953 Dodge pickup truck, a six-cylinder flathead machine, well worn and trustworthy. My parents reasoned that I would be less inclined to risk major road trips with this pedestrian machine. Its rods began rattling at speeds in excess of thirty-five miles per hour. That nullified trips to Portland or other far-flung destinations. After I acquired the truck, the maintenance schedule became oil changes every thirty thousand miles, gas in the tank daily. My buddies and I panhandled dimes and quarters from our fellow high school students to subsidize gas expenses. We hit on a scheme to supplement our allowances and the pittance we earned on odd jobs.

The Arch Cape Shingle Mill

A man named Vic Schultz owned the Arch Cape Shingle Mill down on Arch Cape Creek. Schultz and his crew sliced up cedar logs into shake bolts, sawed the bolts into shingles, and wove the shingles into bundles. Only the most choice, sound slabs of tight-grained red cedar met the standards set by the sawyers for quality shingles. Huge cutoff saws trimmed the bolts of unusable bark and wood fiber. A long conveyor belt carried this discarded material to an enormous cinder cone shrouded in tin. A raging fire consumed the cedar scraps inside this pyre and consigned the smoke to the heavens.

Schultz let locals snatch culled wood from the conveyor as it passed to the firebox. We boys began a massive plan of interception. Gangs of us yanked woodstove-sized chunks from the belt and loaded them into our pickups. We became regulars around the mill yard, eating lunch with the workers and listening to the lore of the mill.

When a truck sagged under a full load of pond-wet cedar, we set out to merchandise the product. Certain glib boys, less sheepish than I, honed their salesmanship skills. We sought out older people. They were often skeptical but softhearted regarding young folks trying to get ahead.

"We're trying to earn a little pocket change for college."

"It's nice seeing young people with initiative."

"Yes, Ma'am, we're trying to make our own way. Can't rely on your folks to give you everything."

"That's good, boys. Is that a full cord?"

"Well, yes, Ma'am, it's real close to a cord."

"It looks kind of wet. Is it seasoned?"

"It's kind of damp right now, but in a couple of weeks, it'll burn like crazy. Guaranteed."

"How much is it?"

"Twenty-five dollars a cord. Stacked."

At this point, we would begin nudging one another in the ribs, chortling to ourselves. We knew we had tenderized the client. Sometimes the nice lady even gave us a few cookies after we stacked the wood. I recall these transactions now with a modicum of shame. We knew that wood would burn quite smartly in two weeks! Guaranteed! Hell, once that cedar dried out from the millpond, a stout fireplace would consume the whole load in two days!

Our best clients were the saintly nuns from St. Mary's of the Valley School. We sold them a shocking quantity of wood to supply their retreat on North Laurel Street. We even coined a new term for our product to commemorate these transactions, "Nun Wood," in honor of their beneficence. If divine justice prevails, I'll perpetually dangle over the flames of Hell for my rascality.

Often entire weekends were spent cutting, splitting, and hauling wood to fill the insatiable maws of wood stove and fireplace. Entire families roamed the woods in pickups searching for likely plots of thinned waste timber. A blithe social atmosphere prevailed. Traveling over the roads behind town, a woodcutter might encounter the Capper family, the Lagerquists, the Nelsons, some Sroufes, Larry Pershin, the Browns. On any weekend, several groups congregated along stretches of the Tolovana Mainline Road, Burn Road, Tillamook Head. We called the area along Burn Road "The Hemlock Mines." Families of itinerant Russian Orthodox thinners from Woodburn cut small hemlock trees and left them lying on the forest floor. Thousands of juvenile trees lay pell-mell on the ground, a vast jumble of pick-up sticks cast over the undergrowth. Families larked about the forest chain sawing and carting wood to waiting pickups. Those were good times. We packed lunches and thermos bottles of hot coffee. On occasions of rare snowfall, we hauled inner tubes and sleds to the hills to test the slopes.

Persh Shows 'Em

Company policy changed in later years. Crown Zellerbach issued permits and restricted incidental waste-wood harvest. We began casting farther and farther east to make up a load. By the early 1980s, most local wood gathering was limited to Tillamook Head and some areas near Saddle Mountain. We persevered. My brother Tim, Larry Pershin—"Persh"—and I took up stump harvest when work got scarce, usually November through March. We'd scratch around all day to cut, split, and load a heaping pick-up. That translated into sixty-five dollars. If we paused for lunch at Flo's Moon Food, our capital diminished frightfully.

Christmas season 1983 hit us hard. On Christmas Eve that year, I had thirty-eight cents in my pocket. Clients had failed payments. Temperatures slipped to the twenties for weeks. We lived on cans of tuna fish, "that goddam cat food," my brother called it. Laughter was scarce, but we hung tough.

I remember one Sunday on Circle Creek. Tim, Persh, and I headed toward a landing above the creek. Persh, a burly man, bald with tufts of red hair shooting out the sides of his head, rode shotgun in our truck. As the acknowledged local wood-splitting champion, his massive trunk and forearms were a welcome addition to any wood caper. Our route took us past another gang of cutters. We nodded cursorily and drove on by, stopping a quarter mile above them on a landing. Tim commenced butchering spruce stumps. Persh and I chased behind him, splitting and sweating in the chill air. A light east wind nibbled at our faces. The day fined up nicely as we established a rhythm.

"Boys," Persh exclaimed, "it's so nice out, I think I'll leave it out!"

Tim stopped to oil the chainsaw. In the stillness of that February afternoon, a voice drifted up to us from the valley below.

"Did you see that big guy in the truck?" one of the cutters asked his buddies. "He looked just like Bozo the Clown!"

I glanced over at Persh. He had obviously heard the cutting remark. A hurt ogre look passed over his countenance. I shrugged at him and continued splitting.

"Humph. Bozo, huh? I'll show them Bozo!"

"Take it easy, Larry, we don't want any trouble."

"I should go talk to them."

"Let it slide."

Larry started whupping the stumps with a vengeance, converting his frustration into a rain of blows on the field of cut logs. In record time, the truck was loaded and down the road. As we passed, Persh glowered at the men like some mean wrestler bent on destruction.

"I guess I showed those punks," he commented.

Splitting Wood as an Art

Splitting wood is an art. Most anyone can chop up green alder or cedar into serviceable firewood, but paring a five- to six-foot round of twisted-grain spruce or fir log is quite another matter. The Art who taught me many of the subtleties was Art Smith.

Art and his wife Audrey lived on the Canadian side at the end of Larch Street. The Smiths were a sweet couple who had labored long and hard with scant reward. They always looked tired, like the struggle to keep even had just about caved them in. The Smiths, in one of life's ironies, were the very people to lend a hand to others. Art joined us on several wood adventures in the waning days of wood gathering.

Art limped painfully. He had sustained a crippling injury at a logging mill. Pausing to loan a fellow worker his rain gear, he had fallen from a

Easter egg hunt and breakfast, Klootchy Creek Park. From left to right: unidentified gentleman, Art Smith, Cleve Rooper, Larry Pershin (Capper Collection)

deck and received injuries that paralyzed him initially and plagued him in later years.

One day he rode along with us to Tillamook Head. We located a huge fir log mouldering away in the undergrowth. Scrabbling around in the salal and ferns, we succeeded in carving up the mammoth with a long-barred McCulloch. We younger guys savaged the first few pieces with a maul and surveyed the disheartening results. A period of maundering and grumbling ensued. Pesky rain began slicking our tools and bodies.

"Boys, this is going to be a long day," someone offered.

Art hobbled over to the log and began inspecting the project. A dissertation on log disassembly followed. Art never issued orders, he merely posed suggestions in a soft voice, then demonstrated the precepts.

"This old fir log has been down seasoning for years. Sometimes you need to analyze a bit before you begin. Look at the pieces you've split. See the grain, real tight, but it's splitting more like spruce than fir. The reason is the twist in it. See the way the grain turns and curves. We'll get her though. Let me see a wedge. Thanks. I'll start here on the edge of this round and open it up across this close-grained section."

Art, barely able to heft the maul, translated the down stroke precisely onto the wedge and a small fissure developed. Deftly he relocated the wedge in just the right quadrant, struggled to lift the maul aloft, and let it drop. A satisfying pop signaled the first dissection.

"Now, one of you boys try it."

We stood in a circle and nodded. When a magician explains a trick, it all seems so simple. That day, I learned a few things about splitting wood. The principles transfer nicely to other tasks in life. Knowing lines of resistance and streams of energy helps surmount the apparently insurmountable. You just need to know where to place the wedge. An elderly man, challenging infirmity, taught me that one dreary afternoon in the foothills of the Coast Range.

Chapter 20
Terrible Tillie Stories

No history of Cannon Beach should fail to include some account of that renowned offshore beacon, the Tillamook Head Lighthouse. I've often snickered over the years when eavesdropping on tourists gazing at the installation from the beach.

"Is that a ship I see out there?" people will query.

"It doesn't seem to be moving much."

In my childhood, the beam it cast on my bedroom wall became familiar as the echo of the sea itself. The winking interval of brilliance and shadow, constant and ceaseless as the waves themselves, made me feel secure, safer somehow, less cowed by the ocean's great maw. Its baying foghorns were a different matter altogether. On occasional hikes to the headland's steep scarp onshore, a day of dank fogs and tree drip could be extremely unsettling. The high reaches of the head itself, an ancient place of spirits and forces, always cast a dark pall on my mood. The trumpeting of the horns on the offshore rock was like the keening of the old gods, the bleating of Baal himself. I've always heard murmurings on that promontory high above the sea, whispers of the primal. The foghorns shivered my daylights and hinted at things best left unknown.

Situated roughly three miles from the village of Cannon Beach and a mile from Tillamook Head, the construction of the light ranks as one of the true engineering marvels of the late 19th century. The grit of those stalwart masons who blasted and hewed the rock and assembled the stone structure beggars the imagination. In the long roll of keepers who

Tillamook Rock Lighthouse, looking southeast to Cannon Beach (Scott Rekate Collection)

manned the light from 1880 to 1957 were heroes and ascetics, misfits and comics. One might as well have been banished to Devil's Island or a parcel on the moon.

My brother and I visited the rock in 1978. On a singularly quiescent sea, still and oily-flat, we nosed his flat-bottomed dory boat onto the only shelf of approach, a section on the eastern rock base. I leapt to the rock as the small boat wallowed in the swell. Local fishermen once called it "the Fly Factory." In late August, clouds of kelp flies breed and swirl above the rock.

Fused to its rock perch, the light and its quarters seem a mere extension of the pinnacle itself. The space constraints are terrifying to behold. "Terrible Tillie" was not a place suited for those with psychic imbalance. The railed area circumscribing the lighthouse scarcely allowed for light calisthenics. A stroll was unthinkable. The mile gulf between our position and the headland seemed a void wider than a leap of faith. How did these men do this? A sense of duty goads men to singular acts of strength and abstinence.

James Gibbs and others have presented fine accounts of the light's history, construction, and occupation. I would refer readers to those publications for a thorough study of the Tillamook Lighthouse story.

Mom Swims to the Lighthouse

I would like to chronicle a few events pertaining to the lighthouse. My mother once swam to the lighthouse from the beach at Seaside, accompanied by an early Seaside lifeguard, Wally Hugg. Wally, Jim Reed, and Bill Palmer worked the Seaside beach during the early golden era of bronzed surf swimmers. Reed and Hugg hailed from Hawaii and swam competitively at the University of Oregon. Terence O'Donnell, a noted Oregon historian, told me that another Seaside lifeguard regularly swam to the lighthouse, engaged the keepers in a game of chess, and then swam back to the beach!

Wally Hugg and his assistants in a Model A Ford, Seaside (Seaside Historical Society)

Gruber and the Lighthouse

My favorite anecdote about the Tillamook Head Lighthouse concerns an enormous German man, one Gruber by name, who made the trip to the rock twice. The party constructing the lighthouse needed a cook. Gruber, a portly man of appetites, ran afoul of these gentlemen in a bar in Astoria. Given to swagger and bluster, he let it be known that he fancied a job on that rock and that the position of cook suited him perfectly. Perhaps the liquor infused him with Dutch courage, one can only surmise. The agents signed him on, requesting that he gather his effects and be prepared to leave on the tender vessel when the weather improved. On the appointed day, Gruber shipped out to the rock. The tender lay off the lighthouse in heavy chop, then eased in to ferry Gruber and another replacement onto the rock.

All exchange of personnel required a breeches buoy and a travelling cable between a tender vessel and the rock. Throughout its many years of operation, this was the most dangerous drill for crewmen and the shuttling keepers. As the tender wallowed and rolled in the maelstrom below the lighthouse, the man in the breeches buoy dangled sometimes high above, or plunged indecorously into the sea.

On this day, Gruber watched as a keeper plummeted several times into the water, only to be wrenched aloft and dunked again.

His pluck failed him, and he returned with the vessel to Astoria, humbled and embarrassed. Tales circulated around the saloons in Astoria. A good deal of cruel ribbing plagued Gruber. One night in the heat of drink and roistering, Gruber vowed that he would "by God, get on that lighthouse" if it was the last thing he did.

True to his vow, he returned to the lighthouse. The tender crew lashed together a makeshift conveyance and trussed up the unfortunate Gruber. He was shunted across to the lighthouse without incident. As the story goes, Gruber never left the light and died in its service.

Retiring the Lighthouse

On September 1957, townsfolk gathered for a wake honoring the decommissioning of our beloved beacon. The U.S. Coast Guard replaced the manned lighthouse with an electronic buoy, automated and unromantic. Families of the village assembled on the beach below Kraemer's Point to mourn its passing. Harley Sroufe and his family supplied groceries for the occasion. Tow trucks hauled an enormous mountain of beach drift logs to assemble a pyre. The blaze lingered long into the night, flames licking into a sky devoid of the beam which had burned for seventy-six years without interruption. The quenching of the light augured the end of an era. All of us stared seaward as the light rotated through its final circuit, winked, and went black. We stood silent for some moments, uneasy and dismayed. On that warm, still, September night, the east winds whirled amongst us, nudging friendly sparks into the air. I remember feeling suddenly chilled and hollow, a stranger in my own home place.

Chapter 21

Surf Lifesaving at the Beach

Any historical account of Cannon Beach should include a substantial section devoted to surf lifesaving. For seventy years, a courageous line of men and women have served vigilantly as surf lifeguards here, wresting swimmers from a chill and hostile sea. Only three Oregon coastal municipalities have formed long-term coastal guarding programs: The City of Seaside, Gearhart, and the City of Cannon Beach. Gearhart abandoned its lifeguards in the seventies, the Ralph Davis family serving for decades as its sole lifesavers. Cannon Beach can be justly proud of its long record of public service.

Our beach has always posed a threat to the unwary. Unlike some ocean beaches, those with gentle shore-break surf and warm water, Cannon Beach's surf character challenges the best of swimmers. The allure of the primordial pool exerts a strong pull on visitors. Longtime head lifeguard Jim Babson once noted that "the tourists flock to the beach like lemmings. They rush headlong into the surf throwing caution to the wind." On Cannon Beach, guard responsibility extends from Chapman Point south to Hug Point. Guards respond to calls in Ecola Park and at Arch Cape when deemed appropriate.

Lifeguard line drill, 1967
(Lindsey Collection)

Long sets of waves crest and peel toward the beach most days, fierce and restless. Rare are those days when the sea whispers and shimmers in passivity. Churn, crush, and surge are the rule. Beach topography contributes to a swimmer's imminent danger. Along the seven-mile strip of beach, headlands and rock outcroppings interrupt the even flow of waves to the land. Small streams flow toward the sea eroding channels in the sand. Flux characterizes the shoreside environs; wind and current shape and reform channels, bars, and beach. Even the most sage beach observers have difficulty reading its features.

A common myth perpetrated for many years was that the surf posed a greater danger when the tide was going out. The notion, apparently, was that the sea would pull swimmers from shore as the tide withdrew. In fact, many swimmers and waders experienced life-threatening perils on returning high tides. In certain beach drainage areas, such as depressions, crab holes, and channels, the sheer volume of water at high tide creates rips or run-outs, strong submarine rivers of water flowing diagonally back to sea counter to wave movement. Unwary swimmers in these rips suddenly find themselves drawn inexorably out beyond the surf line where the current finally dissipates. In most summers of my memory, several rescues occurred at these sites each year. The waders' accounts of the circumstance begin to have a familiar pattern:

"We were just jumping up and down in the waves, and all of a sudden we couldn't touch the bottom anymore!"

The precise location of these dangerous areas changes as the shape of the beach alters. Elk Creek's mouth and the surf line just north of the Ecola Ramp have a long history of active run-outs. Ironically, those two places have enormous congregations of surf bathers every summer.

The First Cannon Beach Lifeguard

The first lifeguard hired in Cannon Beach was Ted Nickelson. Ted guarded alone that first summer of 1938. A wealthy gentleman, Mr. W. W. Ross, promoted the lifeguard program. He had constructed a splendid home on Kraemer Point, now the Sisters of St. Mary's Retreat. Ross, an avid surf bather, swam daily. Ross recognized a need for seasonal lifeguard assistance. He placed small contribution jars in local business establishments and generated public support.

Nickelson lobbied for and was granted assistants during the summers of 1939 and 1940. Two unemployed locals, Clinton Kemhus and Johnny Franklin, assisted him. Nickelson received three dollars a day, and his assistants, two dollars. At roughly one-thousand-yard intervals along the beach, guards placed coils of line with an attached life ring. In an emergency, guards swam the rings to endangered swimmers. Citizens onshore rendered assistance in retrieving the lines. During his employ, Nickelson and his partners undertook four or five rescues. A fisherman swept from Haystack Rock and a couple swimming north of Elk Creek survived. On another occasion, a couple bathing near Haystack Rock encountered difficulties. The girl was saved, the man lost. Nickelson trained in the surf for approximately one half hour a day, swimming without benefit of insulative apparel.

Nickelson set up his post on the beach in front of the old Ecola Hotel. An enormous tree stump had washed ashore and lodged in front of the old building. Nickelson placed a flag atop the stump and opened for business. His personal automobile, a Model A Ford proclaiming "Lifeguard," hastened him to surf emergencies.

"I was in good shape," he indicated.

Ted Nickelson, first Cannon Beach lifeguard, at his post, 1939 (Babson Collection)

I ran the 440 for the University of Oregon track team under the legendary Bill Hayward. One of my helpers, Clint Kemhus, worked in the woods bucking logs. He lifted weights after coming home from a day in the woods. He weighed about 220. He didn't have a

25 years of guarding lives

Lifeguard Reunion, 1979 Front row (left to right): Tim Lindsey, Jay Raskin, Ron Nakata, Al Litwiller, Jim Lilley, Pieter VanDyke, Denis Vaughn Back row (left to right): Ralph Davis, Dick Rankin, Betty Davis, John Spense, Jim Babson, Peter Lindsey, John Alto (Lindsey Collection)

lot of money, so he made his weights out of an old iron bar with concrete-filled buckets on the end. We would train in the surf to adjust to the cold water. Sometimes we'd swim out through the surf north and then come in at Haystack. People would be on the beach watching us. We were hotshots, you know. We had a canvas torpedo buoy with a line attached. We tried using a rope with it, but it was hard pulling it off the beach. In my later rescues, I just attached about six feet of line to the torpedo buoy and it worked pretty well.

I remember that one rescue with the fellow and the girl. We were in the water for about an hour. I suffered from hypothermia. They hauled us, shaking and shivering, up to Ecola Hotel and wrapped us in blankets.

For the first thirty years, attempted rescues were chilling affairs. Fate and the hand of the Almighty played no small part in the success or failure of a rescue event. I witnessed an attempted rescue in the early fifties just off the old Ecola Hotel. Douglas Sage, head lifeguard, swam a large metal torpedo buoy, with attached lifeline, to a distressed swimmer. Volunteers on the beach, in alarm and turmoil, rendered whatever scant aid available. Paul Swigart swam his horse deep into the surf line but failed to reach the victim in heavy surf. I remember an abiding sense of helplessness and

Mac McCoy in his Jeep (Grant/Bartl Collection)

despair. Miraculously, the swimmer survived. Sage returned the victim to the beach, laboring for the better part of an hour in the frigid surf. His young body had a grim purple cast to it, and he shivered uncontrollably. Clearly, these early responses lacked order and training. That would soon change.

Mac McCoy and the New Lifeguard Program

The current lifeguard program, well organized and funded, owes no small debt to its early mentor, Delno "Mac" McCoy. Mac had a hand in most things official. He was fire chief, constable, emergency medical responder, and co-coordinator of the summer lifeguard program. When a rent occurred in the normal fabric of our small-town lives, the first person on the scene was Mac. Mac materialized like a merciful genie, a point rider dashed into action by a siren's wail. Drownings, auto accidents, robberies, fires, and medical emergencies fell within his purview. Mac was always an older man, slightly built and balding. Though never of imposing stature, he was a man of movement, a figure darting wren-like from place to place doing things. One tended to underestimate the force of his presence. Strangers did so at cost. Mac was fearless, guided by a clear vision of mission.

One August afternoon, a caravan of beer goons and hooligans roared up on the beach, staging an impromptu rendezvous and shoot-'em-up. Carloads of whiskified toughs discharged Winchester carbines into the air and threatened vacationers on the beach. A pudgy deputy sheriff summoned to the scene discretely kept his distance and maintained radio contact with superiors.

Then Mac arrived. Dogging his familiar old red Jeep to a halt, he bounded out, sized up the two most formidable wasters, and masterfully disarmed them. The expedition with which he quelled and defused an ugly scene left us all stunned. The handcuffed ruffians babbled and protested, humbled and surprised.

Early Lifeguards and Housing—the Forties and Fifties

During the forties and fifties, guards were barracked at the Cannon Beach Conference Center. Lifeguards, like sailors, have historically evinced a strong swoon factor amongst members of the fairer sex. City fathers hoped the Christian atmosphere and stints of cold-water swimming would diminish the lads' ardor. Prayer meetings and moral suasion kept devilments of the flesh at bay. Predictably, problems developed. One steamy, randy summer, a huge, curly-locked, barrel-chested Afrikaner man hired on as lifeguard. He had a fine Christian bent, slated for missionary work by all accounts. Young conservative Christian girls were all agog. He swaggered about the Conference Center grounds bare chested, flexing, rippling, posing. Clouds of young girls swirled around him, Bibles in one hand, their other hands free to reach out and touch his tanned body. Church elders feared the worst.

At about the same time, another problem compounded the issue of lifeguard housing. One of our finest early lifeguards, Shuji Yamamoto, arrived to assume duties. Hailing from the northern Japanese island of Hokkaido, Shuji swam like a tuna fish in forty-degree water. He effected several heroic rescues under the most adverse circumstances, undaunted by water temperatures that would paralyze most swimmers. Unfortunately, Shuji was a member of that ancient race indigenous to Japan, the Ainu. His teeth were filed to needle points. Given to grinning broadly, his barracuda smile disarmed many people. Worse yet, Shuji wasn't a Christian! He embraced Buddhism or Shintoism or some other heathen worship. He wouldn't be staying at the Conference Center.

Mac solved the problem. After some lobbying, he got the volunteer firemen to share their fire hall quarters with summer lifeguards. Accommodations were spartan, yet comfortable. Mac shepherded his charges like a benevolent Boy Scout troop leader. No drinking, carousing, or hanky-panky on the fire hall premises. Scores of guards found shelter in the old building from the 1950s through the mid-1970s.

As one might imagine, the roster of guards serving Cannon Beach included a wide spectrum of unique characters and personalities. Many were college students destined for notoriety in professional specialties. Dr. Paul Clement (early fifties) attained recognition and respect on the faculty at UCLA as a psychologist. Dr. Steven Subotnick, the "Foot Doctor," went on to edit a monthly column in Runner's World Magazine. As one of the world's leading podiatrists, Subotnick has treated Olympians and the cream of international track and field athletes. When he guarded on our beach, Steve often carted around a satchel of bones, scrutinizing shape and articulation in his spare moments. Pieter Van Dyke and Jim Lilly worked the beach in the 1960s and 1970s and have served the Multnomah and Washington County Sheriff's Departments for decades. Jay Raskin guarded for several summers, living in a makeshift lean-to in the woods above the tower. He now lives in Cannon Beach and practices architecture here.

Chuck Dubois

One of my favorites was Chuck Dubois. Chuck hailed from Blaine, Washington, on the Canadian border. Chuck's rambunctiousness tested Mac McCoy's patience and conservatism. While a student at the University of Washington, Chuck and his roommate, one Sannish by surname, had bumped heads with the university authorities. Chuck and his buddies, campus radicals and coffee house intellectuals, had picketed a Red Cross blood drive, creating quite a stir in the campus district. In that mom-and-apple-pie period, such rakehelly behavior invited wiretap, or

P. VAN DYKE, P. LINDSEY, T. LINDSEY, PATIENT - A. MOREY.

SUMMER 1967. CARRY OF PATIENT IN FROM SURF.

Pieter Van Dyke, Peter Lindsey and Tim Lindsey, 1967 (Lindsey Collection)

an invitation from the House Un-American Activities Committee. Chuck played a booming guitar and caterwauled a fine collection of ribald, anarchist tunes. Dismounting from the lifeguard tower, he would uncase his instrument and serenade the beach with saucy songs of love and political unrest. Staid beach goers of the fifties, accustomed to Eisenhower and Ozzie and Harriet, raised eyebrows. Mac often scolded Chuck gently to little effect. Criticism washed over Chuck like a barnacle at high tide.

Chuck fancied Cruzan Clipper rum. He claimed it as a specific against the frigid waters of our north coast. Carefully packed in his lunch pail, a large thermos contained a decoction of rum and various mixtures to fend off shivers and ennui.

Some mornings, Chuck began testing the sauce before lunchtime. By midafternoon, he was in a fine state, gesturing broadly and nicely primed. At that time, the city provided lifeguards with a well-travelled, yellow '49 Chev' panel truck. The panel had huge, over-inflated balloon tires that sang as the vehicle skimming over dry sand. Chuck slalomed down the beach on patrols like a dust devil, aiming at beach balls and sandcastles. He found unruly dogs particularly irksome. A meddlesome cur snapping at the tires sent Chuck off the edge. Goading the animal, he took the van up to speed, then opened a door to whop it in the backside.

Despite his unorthodox style and blithe spirit, Chuck was a fine guard and endeared himself to us all. He worked rigorously in the surf and took his lifesaving duties seriously. He swam like a turbo-charged porpoise and extracted many potential victims from an unforgiving sea.

In the early sixties, head lifeguard Al Litwiller hired on Jim Babson. Jim Babson became the ironman of Oregon Coast surf lifesaving. For twenty-six years, Jim served as lifeguard at Cannon Beach, rescuing countless swimmers, recruiting personnel, and establishing continuity in the lifeguard program. On one notable occasion, Babson and fellow guard, Steve Subotnick, rescued all five members of a Lake Oswego family in one incident. Upon retirement, Babson received a proclamation designating him "Lifeguard Emeritus" on the Oregon Coast. The formal resolution, citing his courage and service, were read into the minutes of a city council meeting called to honor his efforts. His contributions to the public's safety and welfare were monumental.

The First Woman Lifeguard

The first woman hired as a lifeguard, Gail Schultz (Gabriella Poellek on her arrival from Germany), came to Cannon Beach in the early sixties. Gail, lean, well muscled, and very beautiful, caused a mild ripple in the community. The pattern seems quite familiar to us now, a woman breaking into a profession dominated by men. Would she be strong enough? How would her coworkers respond? Would the community accept her position? Could she command the respect necessary in a position of authority?

I don't recollect any problems associated with this departure from past practice. Gail went about the task quietly and confidently, and that was that. In the past two decades, most summer crews have included a rough balance in the roster between male and female guards. One of our lady guards, Gail Bowen-McCormick, swam the English Channel. Mac McCoy wouldn't have been surprised.

"Ladies don't seem to chill so quickly in icy water," he once told us. "They have indoor plumbing. Indoor plumbing doesn't freeze up so quickly."

The Australian Era in Surf Lifesaving—the Late Sixties

The late sixties ushered in the "Australian Era" in surf lifesaving for Cannon

Beach. In Australia, surf lifesaving is a national passion. Well-organized clubs patrol surf beaches in the great green land of the Southern Cross. These rescue swimmers, the Australian ironmen, attained the status of folk heroes. Two Australian blokes, Tony Knight and Malcolm Cant, well-seasoned veterans of surf lifesaving clubs at Torquay and Maroubra, imported their special brand of surf expertise to the northern Oregon Coast. The two graduate students at the University of Oregon had well-honed skills and wave rapport. After their tenure, other Australians followed them from the University of Oregon, David Knight and Jim Lilly. Beach work served as a pleasant respite from student work-study chores at the university, stacking folding chairs and issuing jock straps at the University of Oregon swimming pool. Mal "Lantern Jaw" Cant had skirmished in that rough and tumble donnybrook, Australian rules "footy." He presented a rather imposing figure shoreside. Both had garnered numerous life saving medals and commendations from Her Majesty, the Queen of England.

Both expressed dismay at the archaic equipment and shaky training procedures for most recruits. On his first surf rescue in Cannon Beach, retrieving a child on a rapidly deflating plastic raft, Mal returned to the beach spewing and raging mad. The reel and lifeline assembly had crumpled into a rusty heap.

"Bloody earth!" he screamed. "This bloody thing is useless! That child was floating out to sea, and his father was asleep on the beach. Didn't have a clue! I had a lash at the idiot. Irresponsible bastard. I should have had a go at him! Lindsey, we've got to get some new gear. This will never do."

I calmed Mal as gently as possible and expressed agreement. Many things needed to be done. In the next few years, much was done.

Funding the Lifeguard Program, Early On

The lifesaving program had operated for decades on a shoestring basis. Citizen contributions funded the program. Guards received a pittance, about one hundred dollars a month. Tony and Malcolm organized the Cannon Beach Patrol, an auxiliary group trained to assist the swimming guards. Additional vehicles supplemented the truck supplied by the city. The patrol staged dances and social events to subsidize the guarding program. Tony ordered a shiny new stainless steel lifesaving reel from the Victoria Surf Lifesaving Association, Australia. A wave of public concern and participation swept north coast beaches. During summer months, Gearhart and Seaside guards joined those from Cannon Beach in discussing standards, training, procedures, and beach safety. Mac's successor, John West, joined with Tony and guard representatives from Seaside and Gearhart in approaching the Oregon State Legislature. Tony and John West addressed the legislature, requesting state funding for Oregon Coast municipalities with surf lifeguards. The legislature approved the request, sharing fiscal responsibility with those communities involved.

Funding the Lifeguard Program, Now

The current Cannon Beach lifeguard program, ably supplemented by the Cannon Beach Fire and Rescue wing, the U.S. Coast Guard Air Station Astoria, and other public agencies, has training and technical assets undreamed of by its pioneers. Communication nets, medical equipment, and modern waterborne retrieval devices are changing the nature of lifesaving.

"I suppose one day we'll be obsolete," Head Guard John Rippey commented to me. "With jet skis and rubber Zodiacs, surf swimmers may become a thing of the past."

I suspect that will not prove to be the case. Surf lifesaving has always entailed apprenticeship, learning the ropes, and seasoning skills in an unforgiving and cranky sea. The catalyst that has held the program together and given it shape is the veteran lifeguard, people like Jim Babson and John Rippey who have devoted years of their lives to recruitment, training, and duty. I surmise that will continue to be the case in years to come.

Chapter 22
The 1964 Tsunami

Whenever I hear our community warning system (COWS) moo on the amplified system, I hark back to 1964 and our only significant tsunami event. During spring break of that year, my buddy Al Litwiller and I were ferreted up in a motel room with a brace of young college coeds. It was a dreary evening outdoors, small rain and wind clattering the aluminum windows in Larson's old motel by the current Surfsand. We lounged around in the musty old room these girls had rented, watching Jack Paar on a black and white television. In 1964, boys had to leave girls by midnight, so Al and I were preparing to make our move, a move home in our case. Suddenly Paar was interrupted by a public service announcement telling us that an earthquake in Alaska had occurred and might precipitate a tidal wave on the Oregon Coast. We walked outside, strolled a block to the beach, and were greeted by a two-to-four-foot standing wave slamming logs and water up the ramp at Bud Stevens' motel!

As we ran back to the motel, old Mac McCoy, our local constable and fire chief, came driving down Hemlock Street in his red Jeep, siren blaring, and told us to hit for high ground, that Silver Point was the evacuation site. Cannon Beach was a very sleepy town in 1964. As old-timers often recall, "You could fire a cannon down main street after sundown and no one would know the difference." Some fifty or sixty souls gathered on Silver Point, chatted, compared notes on what precious keepsakes each of us had brought away with us in this emergency, and generally hung loose.

Elk Creek bridge destroyed by the 1964 tsunami, looking south to school gymnasium (Cannon Beach Conference Center Collection)

After about an hour in a spitting mist and total darkness, a very scary hush settled over the sea. Stepping out of our cars, we could hear sea recession, a very unnerving sensation, something I've never encountered before nor since. The sea simply went away from us and headed for the horizon, sucking all the shoreside debris into its maw. Ten or fifteen minutes elapsed and it headed back, thundering and churning like a whole round house of locomotives. It flailed huge timbers and logs at the base of the point and rattled our underpinnings. Gradually, it resumed its familiar pattern.

The next morning dawned clear and springy. The sea was clean and glassy, horribly transparent and shimmering. It quivered, but generated only one small shore-break wave. In that wave one could plainly discern all the stuff of our lives: sheep and cow carcasses, pieces of boats and pilings, bottles, tree trunks of every species, gas cans, crab floats, light bulbs, garbage, fence posts.

In the aftermath, we fragile mortals surveyed the damage and told our tales. My brother had been partying near Chapman Beach at a bonfire. He headed home to find the Elk Creek bridge washed away. One family rode out the wave in a trailer as it floated up Gerritse Creek on Ecola Park Road. One home drifted off its pinnings and stumbled up Elk Creek. Eighty-six-year-old Emmet Wallis, the world's oldest rock and roll drummer who had recently appeared on the TV program *What's My Line*, was the last to leave town. He had spent the evening at Bill's Tavern and couldn't be persuaded to move.

The town was without water for about a week. Pipe lines had been swept away with the bridge and we were in a fix. The National Guard hauled water to us in tank trucks. June Sweeney ran a tiny lunch room in the old Waves roller skating rink that she called the Peppermint Lounge. In the days that followed "The Wave," her restaurant was one of few in operation. She sold hundreds of her notorious "Bitty Burgers" at 25 cents apiece, peppermint ice cream and homemade pie, and the only restaurant coffee in town. Weeks later she told us about that coffee.

"My boy Hotsie was at home getting ready to take a bath about the time that tidal wave hit. We'd just filled the old bath tub for him. By good luck the tub was still full when all the dust cleared that night. I've been using that water in the tub to brew coffee for the last few days. Pretty lucky, huh?"

I loved those simpler times. Imagine our current crop of tourists sipping triple latte drinks laced with bath water. It makes me smile!

Chapter 23
The Hardy Garbagemen

I expect it's time to take a whack at those hardy souls who cart and si-phon off our unspeakable, the night soil engineers and garbage toters. In pioneer times, all the world was a dumping ground. Homesteaders simply located a convenient depression or streambed close to their cabins and threw cans and bottles into the undergrowth. A tangle of blackberries and salal quickly healed over any clutter or ickiness, and that was that! Once the bottles and bones disappeared in the shrubbery, slipping indecorous-ly from view, they sloughed out of mind as well. In the village of Cannon Beach, a burgeoning population and civic pride dictated some loftier end, an exclusive repository for cast-offs.

A dump was established in the hills northeast of town. The men who trundled waste from homes and cabins were a colorful lot. In my youth, the Elsasser family had locked up the garbage trade. Chris Elsasser owned the franchise and drove truck. His assistant was a young lanky chap named Cliff Hickle. The locals all called him "Dirty Knees Hickle," an endearing jibe, not malicious, because the incessant drip of putrefying garbage scourged his canvas pant legs, indelibly staining the coarse ma-terial. Cliff wore the stains and nickname amiably, a badge of his public service and tribulations.

Our garbagemen served proudly. In what became a village tradition, our garbagemen always possessed a good measure of savoir-faire, a phil-osophical nature, jocularity as a specific against disgust. The men who move garbage form a unique guild. Like members of Masonic lodges, they have special knowledge. Imagine your garbagemen picking through the weekly discards: Oooh la, la—the secrets they discover! A keen garbage-man can read trash like a book. Overdue bills, diapers, old love letters, padded undergarments, girlie magazines, cheap wine bottles, soiled sheets, all reveal volumes. Like high priests they interpret these auguries as commentaries on the nature of life.

Dickie Walsborn took over the route from his stepfather Chris. Dickie ushered in the Golden Age of garbage collection in Cannon Beach. Dick loved a joke, especially a practical joke, and he revelled in trash collection. He called his crew "the G-Men." A long succession of red, hand-me-down vehicles bore the calligraphed title "Miss Cannon Beach." If we were work-ing at some job site, Dickie's arrival signaled a pause in the action. He always shared with us the latest collection of blue stories, jokes, and bits of gossip. As he drove by, he'd yell at us and make a gesture like someone milking a cow.

"How long are you boys going to milk that job?" he'd ask. Dick also initiated the dog treat program. Dick rounded up all the stale loaves of bread he could scrounge from village bakeries and distributed them to the neighborhood dogs on his route. Dogs harbor some sort of innate disgruntlement with garbagemen, and the bread handouts soothed their beastliness.

My favorite garbage story involves Dick and a failed batch of bread dough. Dick got an emergency call late one night from a local baker, Mr. Berger. Dick had neglected to empty the dumpster at the bakery.

"Dick," Mr. Berger's voice spoke excitedly on the phone, "could you come down here quick. I've got a problem in my dumpster."

Dick drove down to the bakery grudgingly.

"When I got there, you wouldn't believe it. A huge mass of fermenting bread dough had filled up the dumpster and was moving down the street! It looked like the Blob that Ate Cannon Beach. If we hadn't hauled it off right then, I don't know what might have happened."

When Dick hung up the route, his son Rich, Jim Malo, and Tommy Misner took over. In their hands, collection became high art and hijinks. The men festooned the garbage vehicle with found objects. When it rum-bled down a graveled side street, the truck looked like some tinker's Gypsy

Tommy Misner with "Miss Cannon Beach," mid 1980s (Misner Collection)

wagon bound for a fair. During one period, the old red truck sported an enormous red lobster on the left front bumper and a large naked doll on the right. Life-size cutouts of The Three Stooges—Larry, Moe, Curly—and Rodney Dangerfield shared the driver's cab. Rodney's head stated a plaint common to garbage guys, "I don't get no respect!" A huge green dragon affixed to the truck licked the air menacingly. These guys wore short pants year round. No can drips on short pants. To lighten the task, the boys would stunt around with your garbage can.

"Better check your can," they'd tell me. "We were by today. That fish you left in there must have been two weeks old! Whew! Paybacks are a bitch."

I'd rush home to find my can hanging high up in a pine tree, with maybe some discarded underwear dangling there too.

Sadly, those times have passed. Some firm in McMinnville quietly and officiously drags off the ruck these days. They appear to lack significant imagination.

Chapter 24
Different Views of Collecting

Thingness and Mr. Leppert

Since we're considering discards, trundling off the junk that accumulates as if by magic in the homes of this great nation, I'd like to make a short observation regarding our love of things. No people in the modern world have gathered such an abundance of material dross and baggage around themselves. Worse yet, we appear to have infected other citizens of the world as well. Even poor tribesmen in the highlands of New Guinea, the "cargo cult" worshippers, dream that cargo plane gods will bring them the stuff that fills our lives. In an economic system premised on production and consumption of goods, acquisitiveness keeps the economy rolling. We wallow in a sty of "thingness," gathering matter around us like dung beetles. In the great material temples of America, Costco, K-Mart, Home Depot, Radio Shack, the faithful cart home truckloads of tin and plastic bloat.

Our predecessors, the northwest coast's indigenous people, conceived of the potlatch, a festival whereby tribal leaders gained status through largesse. Unlike their brothers on the western plains, the Killamooks, Kalispels, and Chinooks lived reasonably sedentary lives. North coast Indians were able to give away material possessions because they simply had plenty, and they stayed where they were.

Squirreling away things has reached epidemic proportions in the late twentieth century. Like pack rats or bowerbirds, we cache away goods in scandalous excess. Perhaps a latent strain of Mormonism or the memory of the Great Depression influences our behavior. In rural Cannon Beach, cannibalized car bodies, wood stashes, and used appliance hoarding were commonplace.

The local Emperor of Thingness was one Mr. Leppert of south Tolovana Park. Leppert owned a rambling, self-constructed manse situated ocean front on Pacific Street. His house was an odd motley of rooms, add-ons, and greenhouses hunched behind an enormous beach rock wall. Leppert toiled for decades on the wall, scouring the beach for round rocks, dragging them home in an old surplus military vehicle. Like Alzheimer's, the collection disease seems to affect the elderly most acutely.

When Leppert died, Ab Childress had some responsibility for cleaning out his nest. Ab dropped by one morning, all agog, to show us the site.

"Boys, you've got to see this to believe it!" he told us. "Stop work, I've got to give you a tour."

We rambled through this Cannon Beach Winchester House virtually speechless. The disease had reached a horribly advanced state.

"Thirty-seven refrigerators! Thirty-seven!" Ab showed us. "Jesus Christ!"

Each room was chuck to bursting with some commodity. Each contained a specialty item. In one, the vinyl siding room, Leppert had stored thousands of scraps and bits of used PVC siding, a rainbow assortment engendering visual vertigo. Another room contained stack upon stack of twelve-inch by twelve-inch carpet samples. The garish swatches, fashionable seventies orange, red, electric green, and avocado, filled virtually every cubic foot. Only a slim filter of light leaked through the piles of carpet from an exterior window.

"Come here," Ab told us. "Wait 'til you see the Pampas Grass Shrine Room! It's unreal!"

At the extreme southwestern wing of the house, one entire room had been given over to dyed pampas grass stalks. In urns, vases, and cans, a forest of dried silky panicles suspired gently in the drafty building. Colored red and green and yellow and orange, the scene induced a creeping nausea.

"My God, Ab. What on earth?" I asked.

"Wait 'til we've finished. There's more. He's set up sorts of shrines in some places. I'll show you the Viking Shrine."

We toured successive rooms with Ab as our guide. One room was entirely devoted to plastic cottage cheese, margarine, and yogurt containers, thousands and thousands, nested together with sacks of lids. Another contained random lengths of plastic and metal rain gutter. Still others housed plumbing fixtures, vitreous china commodes, sinks, water pipes, miles of dimensional lumber.

We coined a term that day to describe this penchant for collection: "Leppertism." As I find myself growing considerably longer of tooth, some early signs of Leppertism, like faint palsy, quinsy, and incontinence, plague me. I exert conscious restraint when large stacks of *National Geographics* or *Reader's Digests* accumulate. I blanch at boxes of rubber bands saved from produce, closets filled with mason jars, green plastic flower pots, aluminum pie tins, bits of string, twine, rope, broken appliances, plastic milk jugs, or sand dollars.

Denny Hyde, Logs and Dogs

Denny Hyde was another famous local collector. He filled his red, white, and blue striped house with cedar logs. Denny also collected dogs, a slack-jawed band of scraggy Beagles, sired by random incest and dissolution. These curs, Gotchew, Chewyou, Bitechew, Pee Wee, Pretty Boy, and Pooper, cohabited with Denny in some uneasy parody of Tom Jones. Denny ran the dogs behind his old pickup truck at dawn. The truck had signs affixed to the body: "Don't drink water. Fish piss in it!" and "Girls Wanted." As the caravan serpentined through town and onto the beach at dawn, Denny caterwauled at them from the cab in a falsetto voice, admonishing them and urging them onward. The sound was unsettling. The whining sing-song borrowed its timbre from the Ozark or Appalachian pig call. Early Sunday churchgoers stood gape-mouthed as Denny hit a high C note and yelled, "Pooper, get your butt over here!"

One late winter day, Larry Pershin was driving over on the north end of Cannon Beach past Denny's house. He described the scene as follows:

Snow lay on the ground. Unusual around here most years. I drove by Denny's red, white, and blue house. I was really surprised to see flowers growing in the snow! I stopped to look. Sure enough. A whole field of colored blooms were growing in Denny's yard. I got out of the truck and walked over to have a good look. When I got closer, I realized the blossoms were actually wads of pastel toilet paper! Someone had wiped up piles of dog manure with the tissue, and then thrown them out into the snowy yard! Looked just like a field of spring flowers.

Chapter 25
The Picards

The chapters of my life have always been punctuated by Picards. The Picards are an old-growth family in these parts. Generations of Picards toiled in the adjacent woodlands setting chokers, rigging, falling, chasing gear on the landings, and generally working doggedly to extract intractable stands of timber and cellulose matter out of Clatsop County forests. My peers: Frank, Roland, Bobby, Marie, Paulette, and Danny have labored tirelessly at entry level jobs for decades.

Frank, Roland, and Bobby held jobs with Crown Zellerbach Corporation which operated in our Coast Range foothills for years, finally succumbing to financial pressures. The owners told them early on that there were only two kinds of employees—the fast and the dead. Spar trees had to be one hundred and ten feet high, the choker cables that hauled the logs back on high lead operations an inch to an inch and a half woven cable.

They hacked away at the trees during the day, rode the crummy out of the woods after an arduous and dangerous shift, and proceeded to slake their dry throats with spirits. When the proper level of therapy was attained, the guys sought out a suitable scuffle. This was a daily ritual. A donnybrook capped the end of most perfect days. If an offender of appropriate stature and demeanor couldn't be located, they squared off against one another and let the skin and whiskers fly.

Roland described one evening from his Bridge Tender Tavern days. The barmaid refused to serve a knot of restless loggers, not an uncommon event by all accounts. The faithful gathered her up, strapped her to the top of the pool table, and served themselves.

Sometimes lathered up loggers would exit the Bridge Tender by leaping from the adjacent Broadway Street Bridge into the Necanicum River, there to flounder around for a bit.

The patriarch of the Picard clan was Jesse, a genuine bear of a man. He gained status in our local logging hall of fame as a consequence of an accident in 1978. Jesse fell while "chasing" on a landing. A loaded log truck, driven by Orville Jones, ran over Jesse in his bed of soft soil. In order to extricate Jesse, the truck had to back up and roll over his body again. Doctors feared his imminent death at the hospital, not an infrequent occurrence in the logging profession. He lived, spent nine months in a body cast, and miraculously recovered. For the rest of his life, he moved with a rolling limp.

Let there be no doubt. The Picards are tougher than most of us. Impervious to normal pain, buffalo strong and wiry, undaunted by driven rain and screaming wind, they test the bounds of mettle. I want a Picard with me in a street fight.

For years, the taverns and lounges had a "Three Picard Rule." No more than two male Picards could be in an establishment at any one time—and if three showed up together, one had to leave. The Picard women were exempt.

Roland and Frank currently trundle off trailer loads of detritus that collects in people's cottages and homes. Driving a parti-colored stable of old homemade trailers and bastardized trucks of questionable parentage, the lads operate their scrapping and hauling business under the name Over the Hill Hauling & More. Refrigerators, freezers, rotten wood, roofing, pianos, defunct appliances of all kinds, unmentionable caca, all find their way to the dump via Picard hauling. No job seems too daunting for these gents. Of a Friday evening, following an exhausting work week, we gather for a barley pop at Cheri's Café and sidle over to the nearby distillery for a small tot of rum.

"Boys," Frank will say, tipping a glass of the amber liquid back, "I feel the Power Juice beginning to work!"

"Hawhoooa!"

Frank Picard Has a Drink at Oney's

On one memorable evening when the juice was loose, Frank held court at the Cannon Beach Distillery. The Brothers Picard were staging for The Night of Fire, an explosive evening of drag racing at the Woodburn Drag Strip in Woodburn, Oregon. Frank, amped and cranking over at six thousand RPMs, described this incident:

We were working a logging side up near Elsie. After a tough week, we dropped in to Oney's Restaurant for a little refreshment. Nygaard's boys were in there and plenty of Crown Z loggers too. About forty-five of us altogether. We heard a roar outside. The Gypsy Jokers had showed up. They wandered in, wearin' rebel flags and other biker shit. Things began to get a little bit tight in there and we smelled trouble. Three of them went outside to have a smoke.

Oney, she was quite a gal. You remember. She sets a shotgun on the bar. Twelve gauge. Both triggers back. Drinkin' whiskey out of her coffee cup. We loggers are thinkin', "All right you Jokers. Make that move!"

One of our guys had slipped out to the crummy. He fired up one of our chain saws and busted through the door! Blade spinnin'! You should have seen those mothers run.

After they'd all left, Oney says, 'How many of you are carryin'?' Everybody had weapons.

"Put 'em away," she said. "I'll buy a round."

"I ain't dead yet," Frank likes to tell me. "I've got abusive endurance!"

Chapter 26
Realty and Reality

The natural charms of Cannon Beach have made property in the environs a valuable commodity from the earliest days of settlement. Owners and agents recognized its worth and sought to develop tracts of "sylvan glades" and "fabulous ocean viewscapes." As the prime oceanfront property dwindled, phrases like "a peek of Haystack Rock" or "near the beach" appeared in sales brochures more frequently. Eddie Beers coined the term "land maggots" in reference to our realty contingent. Early survey lines meted out parcels in hazy fashion. Current owners evince surprise when they find their homes located in city streets or their bedrooms firmly planted in a neighbor's yard. In a kinder world, a rigid code of ethics would prevail.

Billboard, Highway 101 south of Cannon Beach (Cannon Beach Conference Center Collection)

Kent Price and George Frisbee operated real estate offices in the early village. Stories circulated about Mr. Frisbee, a shortish amiable gentleman, and what came to be known as "Frisbee's Whale." When George took prospective buyers to view a piece of property close to the ocean, he liked to impress them with the natural wonders they could expect to see in the ocean adjacent to their property. A rock pinnacle sits south and west of Haystack Rock. Waves surge across this wash rock rising from the ocean floor. "And look!" Frisbee would point out for clients, "we have whales in the ocean here just offshore. You'll be able to see them from your living room." People began to call the wash rock "Frisbee's Whale."

Dean Bonde sold real estate here for several years during the seventies. He liked to tell this realty story when a collection of locals gathered for a beer in the evening:

I was a real estate agent here when Oyala and Niemela drifted into town. [Jim Oyala and Jim Niemela purchased business property in Cannon Beach, including the Ratskeller Tavern, Simon's Seashore Restaurant, and adjacent property.] Oyala came first, looking desperately for a place to stay. I knew where a little cabin was available. Small, mind you, and a bit drafty, but cute. Had a real nice little quarter-moon window in the front door. A one-room beach cottage. Well, Oyala moved in. I drove by a few days later. Saw a TV antenna stickin' out of the roof. I stopped to say hello and see how he was gettin' along. Oyala said he was real cozy in there. Couple of days later I drove by again. I saw two TV antennas stickin' out of the roof. I knocked on the door. Oyala answered my knock. "Say Jim," I said, "I was just drivin' by and I noticed two TV antennas on your roof. That seemed peculiar to me."

"Oh," he told me, "I forgot to tell you. I subleased the basement to Niemela."

Chapter 27

Police and Firemen, on the Job

I'd like to take an oblique glance at those public servants, the police and volunteer firemen, who maintained community order and safety. Prior to the early fifties, if a ructious bar fight, burglary, or dead body disturbed the normal flow of daily events, one contacted the county sheriff in Astoria or the Oregon State Police. Mac McCoy, deputized and operating as de facto constable, handled later disturbances of the public good. A gentleman named Nick Rubin, retired from a nightstick beat in Portland, hired on as our first official city policeman in the late fifties. He patrolled the township in an enormous gunboat Mercury convertible, circa 1957. With no police station, no formal uniform, no radio, and no municipal judge, he sculpted the few city ordinances to suit himself. He periodically bullied a stray dog or counseled an aged, unruly drunk. Nick, a portly man of relaxed inclination, left the heavy stuff to the sheriff. He mostly walked and chatted up folks on Hemlock Street.

Following city incorporation, a move necessitated by the need for a sewer system, the city hired a mild, personable young man, John West, as its first police chief.

John practiced his own gentle brand of police discretion. He quickly won the community's trust. John went by the book, but he sometimes tore out a few pages if common sense or compassion dictated leniency. John had a keen sense of humor, a damn fine quality in any peace officer. John recognized the flawed and foibled nature of the human animal and cut some slack when necessary. A few incidents should serve to illustrate his modus operandi.

During one particularly harsh winter in the mid-sixties, the hippie woodcutters in town had been hard pressed to find stove wood to heat the beach cabins they inhabited. John received a complaint citing wood pile theft. John knocked on Larry Pershin's door in response. A nice veneer of snow lay on the ground.

"Larry," John began, "your neighbor claims you've been taking wood from his wood pile."

"What makes him think I'd do that?"

"Now, Larry," John continued, smiling a wry grin, "come with me for a few minutes. I want to show you something. You sure you haven't been taking wood?"

"Oh, no."

John led Larry out into the yard. A clear string of footprints engraved in the snow led from Larry's cabin to the neighbor's house.

"Uh, I guess I'll take some wood over to him," Larry offered.

"Thanks, Larry. That's generous of you. I guess this case is closed."

On another occasion, a bird was discovered captive in a summer cottage. John was out of town. An officer responded in his absence, secured a key, and freed the captured bird. The officer left a note for the owner on a kitchen table. John returned to duty. An angry, hostile letter had been received from the disgruntled homeowner, criticizing John and the rude and foul-mouthed officer in his department. Bewildered, John confronted his patrolman.

"I let the bird out," he replied. "Then I left a note. I can't imagine what's the matter."

Girding himself up for the worst, John visited the homeowner. She produced a penciled note, roughly scrawled on a sheet of newsprint, as follows:

I LET THE LITTLE FLICKER OUT. OFFICER ——-.

The way the letters oozed together explained the misunderstanding. John tried unsuccessfully to placate the offended party. I guess police work has its downsides.

Cannon Beach's volunteer fire department was not always the finely tuned organization one encounters today. In a time past, long before pagers and radio communication, a substantial siren perched atop the old fire station on Spruce Street. Volunteers scrambled to the old block building when the alarm sounded, dogs baying and gravel flying from the tires of volunteers' trucks. Assembled, they donned an odd assortment of boots, black helmets, and canvas gear, then posted off to the fire site. Most of the remaining citizenry, if ambulatory, also scurried to witness a fire. Fires had a perverse way of catching on during the small hours. Cedar shingled houses and faulty wood stoves made for nasty fire storms. Most single family residences burned to the foundation, a glowing incarnadine patch in the night sky.

A few fire calls had a lighter side. In the early fifties, the department responded to a call from the Cannon Beach Conference Center. A passerby had heard a loud voice calling "fire" and some other indistinguishable phrases. Firemen dashed across the street to the Conference Center grounds. Gathered on the grass near the chapel, the firemen discovered a prayer meeting in progress. A particularly rabid Pentecostal, deep in the throes of sermonizing, had flayed his flock in stentorian voice, castigating them for sin and shamefulness. They would dangle in the pit of hell, he warned them, and roast in "fires of damnation." Mild confusion and embarrassment greeted the fire squad on arrival.

By the mid-seventies the general complexion and appearance of the firemen had changed dramatically. The older guard, mostly tidy and retired gentlemen of quiet demeanor, had been supplanted by a younger, bushier-haired set of free spirits. A fire department photo from this era would include the likes of Cleveland Rooper, called "Chief" by his cohorts because he was low man on the totem pole, Tim Hersha, Bob Gilmore, and John Merrill. In full beards and fashionable shoulder-length hair, these firemen looked like buffalo hunters fresh from a drunken jamboree, a gang of Hells Angels in firemen suits.

I remember a fire call from about this time in the neighborhood. A little spinster lady had a chimney fire. I ran next door as the firemen arrived. As they charged through the yard, the poor woman had an ashen face. Her expression, wide-eyed and fearful, told everything. These young men sent to save her property looked like a tribe of Mongols bent on rap-

Fire aftermath, cabin on N. Larch Street (Amos Collection)

ine and savagery. Dark and shaggy, they conjured up horrible images in the hearts of some citizens. They worked together with a will and quickly staunched the flames.

Despite a rough appearance, the department quickly established a reputation for competence and professionalism. At about this time the Cannon Beach Rescue Squad began training emergency medical technicians. Many of these young volunteers were in the first wave of trainees skilled in rendering first aid and first response treatment.

Despite the gravity of their calling, some incidents had a distinctly comic quality. One in particular comes to mind. The Cannon Beach Fire Department arrived at a recently remodeled home, called on a report of a chimney fire. The occupants vacated the residence after lighting a fire in the new wood stove. Smoke choked the rooms causing the occupants to flee. Firemen scaled the building to the roof searching for the offending chimney. After a hasty search, the men climbed down the ladders to the ground. No chimney on the roof! Searching the premises, the squad discovered the problem. The chimney only extended into the attic! The contractor had neglected to tell the owners that the chimney hadn't yet penetrated the roof!

On a darker side, the worst single residence fire in Oregon history, at the time, occurred one night on the Canadian side of Elk Creek. A young mother and her four children burned to death in a tiny cabin on North Larch Street in 1963.

Chapter 28
Surfing

Coastside sports and recreation have always played a prominent part in Cannon Beach life. Boats, World War II amphibious "ducks," inner tubes, canoes, and kayaks splashed through the surf over the years. Round plywood discs called Pypo boards found favor with beach bathers. Balsa and fiberglass surfboards appeared in the early sixties. The earliest surfboards on our coast were carved planks or frames covered with canvas. A small number of early surfriders had ridden waves during the forties on southern Oregon beaches and at Seaside. Ralph Davis, veteran Gearhart lifeguard, has photographs of himself riding a board in Seaside in the forties and fifties.

North Shore Surf Club patch (Mekenas Collection)

The surfing storm hit Cannon Beach in earnest by the early 1960s. The hub of north coast surfing during its formative years was Indian Beach, a special place, a secret place, every surfer's dream. Before the advent of neoprene wetsuits, surfing was a summer thing. A small band of cognoscenti gathered on the round rock beach south of Tillamook Head to test the waters during summer months and the sweet days of early autumn. These early surfers were the envy of local youngsters. The wizardry of wave riding cast a spell on those youth that persisted and grew. Those of us who were ocean timid or too poor to buy a board dreamed of joining in, paddling out to sea, gathering around the fire with surfing locals, and fielding questions from young ladies enraptured by the sport.

Rarely more than a dozen in number, this fraternity of young men laid the groundwork for a tsunami wave of surfing popularity. Watchers hung out on piles of driftwood logs, entranced at the young water mystics who slid down steep green gradients, larking and hollering at the sky.

The Beach Boys, in a popular song of the day, sang of safaris, journeying into unknown territory. In those summer days of 1959–60, ragged old pickup trucks and vans wound down a heavily wooded and isolated gravel road to Indian Beach. At the end of that road was a sheltered cove, very quiet and isolated. In the earliest years, only a few people knew what transpired there. The inner circle included some of the following: John Spence, a darkly handsome Seaside lifeguard; Dana Williams, an early board shaper from Southern California; Dick Wall; Roy Parnell (called "Hoedun" by his buddies); John Alto; Jim Sagawa; Mike Zalk; Paul Bernick; and others.

The boards themselves were enormous fiberglass planks, big and wide as sidewalks, nine to ten feet long. Most drifted in circuitously from California: Velzies, O'Neills, Cons, Bings. Reinforced with redwood and balsa stringers midboard, the earliest had long skegs, hard shaped fins like sailboat keels. Most riders knee paddled to reach the pocket, the breaking area, where surfers gathered together in the lineup.

The headlands surrounding Indian Beach funneled huge piles of drift logs on the round rock shelf. The surfers, after lumbering down the trail with heavy boards, set about the first order of business, building a huge fire. Most surfers wore cutoff Levi pants and a T-shirt. More fashionable surfers had a pair of "Jams," a baggy, long-legged set of shorts. When the fire was roaring nicely, the boys entered the chill water for a short session. Water temperatures often dropped to forty-eight degrees Fahrenheit. Purple lips, involuntary quaking, and acorn-sized testicles brought the lads back to the fire.

Dick Wall gained a reputation for his special concoction, a homemade mead drink, that fended off chills. Bottled in Safeway soft drink bottles, the stuff sang in the veins and loosened tongues. His surfing buddies called him "Cragmont," a Safeway trade name for its soda pop.

None of the boards had leashes. Losing a board generally entailed a swim to the beach. Youth, vigor, and bravado kept the surfers pumping for a speedy return to the water. Some great characters materialized. A beefy footballer named Ron Glover showed up occasionally. Ron chewed twelve ounce Olympia beer bottles into glass shards and swallowed them. Bonfires and ukulele sing-alongs capped a fine day in the sea.

"I feel like Peter Pan," John Spence told us one September day as a smooth east wind peeled spindrift off perfect green waves, waves lined up like ruled notebook paper. "It's like I'll never have to grow old. We're in Never Never Land here." I guess soaring on water is like that.

Vince Morrison operated the first surf shop in Cannon Beach. The slender shop occupied the south end of the Waves Roller Rink, an area now used as a costuming and dressing room for the Coaster Theatre. A very slim space, barely eight feet wide, extended the full length of the building. When Vince took over the space, he began clearing out decades of stored items, mostly old movie posters: Laurel and Hardy, Orson Welles, Lana Turner. Vince ran the tiny shop for several years at that location. Peter Adamson, Jim Sparks, and David Louis opened the next shop. In the late sixties, the old Log Cabin Restaurant, run by Nellie Koonce, went out of business. The boys set up their surf shop in 1967 inside the old log building, carrying an extensive line of Haut surfboards.

Floating devices had been illegal in the surf on Cannon Beach under city ordinance. In 1967 the Cannon Beach lifeguards approached the city council and asked that a specific surfing area be established just south of The Needles. The council agreed. Two large poles, striped in bold primary colors, delineated the area. The council expressed some fear that the surfers might face dangers in the surf. Time has proven that not to be the case.

Thousands of surfers of all ages and genders have tested the waters in, and adjacent to, Cannon Beach in the past forty years. For the past three decades, Cannon Beach has been home for a true regional surf legend, our own Jack Brown. Jack Brown retired in Cannon Beach in his mid-fifties and began surfing daily to retain flexibility in his back. At eighty years,

Jack Brown (Lexie Hallihan Collection)

Jack surfs virtually every day. As any local surfer will attest, Jack is not simply a fair-weather surfer who rides the soupy waves in shore break. Jack mixes it up with the best of them. Undaunted by frequently foul weather, Jack joins the boys in the lineup on all but the heaviest days. Some surfers are cranky, selfish of their personal spots, territorial. Jack disdains that sort of attitude. Scores of young surf riders have benefitted from Jack's surf savvy and expertise. Many a novice surfer has learned the ropes from Jack. Countless old boards and wetsuits have passed from Jack's hands to young would-be wave riders. A shy, gentle man, quick to smile, Jack has long been my hero and idol. With grace and dignity he has linked himself with primordial force, riding for decades down those long undulating sea lines toward infinity.

Chapter 29
The Dory Fleet

I was called Peter after Simon Peter, the fisher of men's souls. My family's life has been inextricably linked with fishes and water. Never have I lived farther than a mile from the sea, and my life, like Norman Maclean's, has been "haunted by waters": streams, lakes, boats, fishes, and the sea. Thoreau said, "Time is but the stream I go a-fishing in." I understand that. I have never been a hunter. Hunters confront their quarry eye to eye. I prefer penetrating the shimmering envelope that separates fish from fisher, known from unknown. I like fishing the ocean void, hoping to land answers to elusive questions. I would like to tell something of the nature of fishing the Upper Left Edge from a dory boat in the late 1970s.

Our coastline once supported a substantial industry based on the commercial harvest of troll-caught salmon. Commercial salmon trolling, like the species sought, has become something of an anachronism. In 1978 I joined the commercial dory fleet, grasping at the industry's flukes as it took its final dive.

Stealing winter hours from my teaching duties, I outfitted the bare hull of a Clipper Craft dory. She was twenty feet long from bow to stern, lap-strake built, square of transom, and slender as a reed. Her antecedents harked back to New England and the Old World, doughty double-ended vessels both sailed and rowed. East Bank double-enders ploughed the cod grounds, ubiquitous as menhaden, a mainstay of fishing life and history. My boat, The Schmedlow, was fashioned of deep auburn wood, Bristol bright on her flat, blue bottom, petticoat white in the laps, pert, fresh, and

Dory coming through the surf, The Needles in the background (Lindsey Collection)

trim. West Coast "West Bank" dories generally rely on the square stern for attachment of motors or outdrive propeller units. The addition of a seventy horsepower outboard motor gives the West Bank models the power needed to punch through ocean surf.

Please join me for a short day trip working the twenty-nine fathom line just west of Tillamook Head Lighthouse. We'll target the June coho salmon, huge silver ribbons of fish streaming toward coastal rivers. As a reader, you can make the trip in your mind's eye and avoid seasickness. Like my old dory fishing friend Eddie Beers on The Tickler, I often fished alone.

"Pack a big lunch," he'd say to occasional passengers, "and I'll eat it when you throw up." He virtually guaranteed nausea. After his dory's run to the fishing grounds, he would slow to troll speed and commence sucking on a frozen herring like a kid slurping a popsicle.

The Cannon Beach Dory Fleet traditionally launches its boats just south of The Needles, a pair of sea mounts just south of Haystack Rock. Before first light, the fleet's trucks and boat trailers—scruffy, rusty, scaly—collect at Haystack Rock for launch preparation. Troll poles are lowered and motors tested. Hot tips on where "the bite" is expected are shared and considered. Lure discussions follow. Should we rig up Dory Demon

Tim Lindsey, Peter Lindsey, Eddie Beers, and a string of salmon (Scott Rekate Collection)

Hoochies with Glo-Glo centers or Laundromat Hoochies? The latter received its name because a dory fisherman in our fleet once met a cute girl at the laundromat in Pacific City the same day he caught a boatload of fish. Hoochies are small plastic squid-shaped lures. Testimonials touting one lure or another and fish talk continue on the beach and persist all day over CB radios onboard each boat—a practice called "radio fishing" by sarcastic high-line fishermen.

As dawn arrives, the dories are cast from their boat trailers into the surf line, and the dicey business of negotiating the skittish, flat-bottomed vessels through the surf commences. Many dory trips begin and end with this launch into the breakers. For many years, dark dreams plagued me after my boat, The Schmedlow, swamped at the outside Needle. On The Schmedlow's maiden launch, my girlfriend Hazel and I nosed the dory out to sea. Suddenly the surf became silent. I looked forward into a ten-foot wall of green glass, angled over the mast and running lights. The advancing wave caved in, a lime green avalanche ripping and dismembering trolling poles, gas cans, console, windshield, tackle trays, and gear. I watched the water yank Hazel's head backward and tear off her stocking cap and glasses. The boat filled to the gunwales in seconds, thirty-pound lead cannon balls rolling about, gas cans sloshing at our feet, hooks, flashers, and salmon plugs swirling threateningly around our legs. The motor and electronics failed immediately. After a few moments, the waves abated and we drifted slowly to the beach, humbled and chastened.

Once the short surge through the surf has been negotiated, the boat begins its run to Tillamook Head Lighthouse. The trip of several miles is accomplished rather quickly in a dory. Dories are tenacious sea vessels, hardy and durable.

My most successful trolling occurred in rip lines formed just outside the lighthouse. A plenitude of pinnacles rise from the ocean floor near the rock and its lighthouse. Long currents dredge up phytoplankton from the depths in lines that extend for miles quite distinctly. Fish feed voraciously in rips. Here we dorymen lowered our cannon ball weights and a multitude of "spreads" (leaders and lures attached to four stainless steel lines). Thirty or more lures flip and flash through the water at various levels from the surface to twenty or thirty fathoms below. Most dory trollers affix bells to the tips of their two trolling poles that jingle when fish hook themselves.

All day we ply the waters on a north-south tack, tiny midgefly boats hatched on a June sea. At dusk perhaps forty or fifty silver salmon (coho) and a "smiley" (Chinook salmon) or two nest in the fish box.

We pull our gear and head for the beach, Haystack Rock prominent to the southeast. From the seas west of Cannon Beach, the verdure of the foothills tumbling to the beach beggars description. The land claims us until tomorrow's launch. We pray for fair winds and a following sea.

A peak moment in my early life occurred one sparkling day in August, 1979. My brother Tim, an Australian John Druce, Hazel, and I visited Tillamook Lighthouse by dory boat. Tim's stout fiberglass dory skimmed to the lighthouse over oily slick seas. Upon arrival, he nosed the vessel onto the east rock ledge and we jumped free. Few have had that privilege, and I cherish that experience.

Chapter 30
Early Castles in the Sand

The early sixties brought another activity to Cannon Beach. It began innocently enough. In 1964 a lady named Billie Grant started a program of children's activities during the summer months. In the southern wing of Sroufe's Grocery (current site of Osburn's Ice Creamery), Billie organized projects for young people: weaving, beach rock painting, craft work, puppetry. Billie, with encouragement from other craft people in the community, Bill Steidel principally, decided to take her young charges to the beach for a day of freestyle sand sculpting. On the appointed day, a local excavation contractor scooped up a huge pile of sand oceanward of the Ecola Ramp. The kids, assisted by Billie and Bill, fashioned an enormous dragon from the mound of sand.

The sheer fun of sand moulding caught on quickly. By the following year, a full-blown contest, replete with plastic sand bucket prizes and gift certificates, sat center stage on the wet sands of Cannon Beach. Organizers selected the lowest tide sequence of the summer season, meted off plots of sand, then stood back while entrants bucketed, shaped, and dug hundreds of cubic yards of sand. Teams participated, gangs of children dug in, members of the press materialized at events, word spread far and wide. Artists and craft people from the community judged contestants on merit and theme. Like Harriet Beecher Stowe's character Topsy, it just grew. By the late sixties, huge crowds bloated the sleepy resort community and threatened public safety.

The annual event, now formally called the Cannon Beach Sandcastle Contest, proudly displayed a yearly poster rendered by a local artist. An

Betsy Bamford and Deenie McKennon and their winning sandcastle, 1965 (Lackaff Collection)

annual souvenir T-shirt bore an imprint of the official sandcastle poster. Merchants revelled in the additional tourist influx and welcomed the chance to cadge a few dollars from increasing hordes. Many visitors who had no previous knowledge of the community arrived and recognized its natural charm and splendor.

The sandcastle contest had its lighter side too. In its first few years, Frank Lackaff often served as a judge. Many members of the vast Lackaff clan summered in Cannon Beach. Frank had been fervently courting one of the McKennon girls, Deenie McKennon. Both Deenie and a clutch of Lackaffs were entered in the same category. When the awards were presented, Deenie and her friend Betsy Bamford won first prize. In the aftermath, one Lackaff, Frank's brother Freddie, was prompted to comment on the outcome.

"It just goes to show you," he opined, "sex is thicker than blood!"

Chapter 31
Live Music at the Beach

The performance of live music has long been a significant recreational diversion for the residents of this coastal community. Ma Gerritse describes early dances at local homesteads in her journal:

"We would meet at some cabin and dance all night sometimes. Someone would play the fiddle and sometimes there was an accordion. It was at one of those parties that I met John [her future husband]. He used to stop sometimes along the way [his mail route] and dance all night. Imagine a man waltzing in rubber boots!"

The Presbyterian Church and the Conference Center often featured guest soloists. Big bands performed in Seaside dance halls like the Bungalow. The Waves Roller Rink held dances on Saturday nights. Paul Swigart, proprietor of the Sea Ranch Stables, often serenaded horseback riders returning from night rides with his saxophone. Beach boys strummed guitars and ukuleles around beach fires.

The Invasion of Paul Revere and the Raiders

In the sixties, musical performance careened off in a slightly different direction. A conservative element directed public policy in Cannon Beach during the early sixties. The town was a sleepy place and the city fathers exerted a subtle moral suasion on its young people.

One August afternoon, a cortege of unusual automobiles rolled slowly into town and halted at the Waves Roller Rink. The cars were vintage hearses, dark Cadillacs. Printed in bold letters on the sides of one vehicle were the words "THE RAIDERS." Debarking from the machines, an odd gang of young men stretched their legs and surveyed the weathered store fronts. Several had shoulder length hair or wigs. They were dressed in strange tunics, waistcoats, and looked like displaced Minutemen two hundred years out of time. Most evinced a certain hauteur, peering out through dark glasses at the quiet street. Their facial expressions suggested that they hoped to be elsewhere.

The young men commenced dragging boxes and instruments into the old skating rink. The word that day blew through town like a gust of southwest wind.

"They're a band. From Idaho, I heard."

"What're they called?"

"The Raiders. Paul Revere and the Raiders. They dress up like British Redcoats. It's rock and roll. They're playing at the Waves on Saturday night!"

The city fathers were not enchanted. The city council held a special emergency session to discuss the impending concert. Councilmen voiced grave fears. One councilman aired his displeasure: "I don't think we want Sam and the Red Hots playing in our town! What will become of the children?" To their credit, the council voted to allow the music to proceed, barring unnecessary noise or public disturbance.

By Saturday night clouds of young people descended on Cannon Beach. The rumble of bad exhaust systems and high-pitched catcalls filled the quiet streets. At eight o'clock the old wood building wobbled and thumped, swollen with teenagers. The sheriff, his deputies, and the Oregon State Police hovered around and on premises. When Mark Lindsay of the Raiders teed off on piano for the opening number, the young people erupted into a churning mass of movement. A groaning baritone saxophone and thunder drums hurled bolts of sound into the night air. Rock and roll had arrived in Cannon Beach. For his closing number, Mark Lindsay hung from the rafters of the old skating rink and bellowed out "I'm gonna wait 'til the midnight hour, when your love comes tumblin' down..."

Rumors circulated the following day. The band staged an after-hours party. Beer flowed freely. Minors had participated. Young people stripped

(Cannon Beach Conference Center Collection)

naked on the beach, coated themselves with Crisco Shortening and slithered around wantonly, dancing with wild abandon in the moonlight. Truth is a shape shifter. Regardless of the facts, rock and roll landed hard in Cannon Beach. In succeeding years, groups like the Kingsmen, Don and the Good Times, and Big George and the Corvettes twanged and rumbled through Cannon Beach. The Swigarts hosted several musical aggregations at their Keg Room on Elk Creek: The New Tweedy Brothers Vocal and Instrumental Band, The Sage Brothers Band, and Teddy and the Roughriders.

The Homegrown Dance Hall

In 1969, Tony Knight and I rented a substantial warehouse on Dawes and Hemlock. We dubbed the cavernous hall "The Barn" and fitted it out for musical performances and dancing. The counterculture at Haight and Ashbury Streets in San Francisco set the tone for our interior decor and band selection. We spread word around town that the building would house regular rock and roll dance action. We elected to decorate the interior walls spontaneously. On a specific evening just prior to Memorial Day, we invited young people in the community to show up for an "Art Happening." We purchased gallons of paint spanning the broad color spectrum. A gaggle of eager teenagers stormed the building on the appointed night ready to wield brushes. What ensued was a full-tilt, no-holds-barred paint-in. Walls, chairs, counters, ceilings fell prey to the amped-up imaginations of countless young people. Tony and I draped an enormous parachute over the ceiling of the hall. We wanted dancers to feel they'd entered a place like Samuel Coleridge's pleasure dome.

By Memorial Day we poised in readiness, like two gentlemen holding a gunny sack, waiting for a snipe hunt to begin. A dark and dulling rain cooled our spirits. We had invested $300 on a psychedelic band from Eugene, the Palace Meat Market. Their musical prowess and drawing power were unknown commodities. Early that morning an advance contingent of band members arrived, two shaggy, vacant-eyed youths.

"We love Coltrane," one offered. "We rock his stuff, man."

The other, a scraggle-haired mock-Jesus summed up his biography thus: "I have my drugs and my drums. That's all I need in life."

We fretted. Our fears were not ill-founded. That night a slim gang of teenagers hung listlessly around the hall's perimeter trying to identify with the dissonant yawp and clangor assaulting their minds and ears. The band featured a light show, a swirling vortex of projected colors and 8 mm movie film featuring a hairy man bludgeoning a television set to death with a broad axe. The young people were not impressed.

"We can't dance to that noise!" many told us.

We parlayed next day and changed strategy. We polled the kids.

"Hire the Washington Merry-Go-Round," they told us. We did. For two months they tooted and strummed and packed our hall. Local boys, the Merry-Go-Round drew immediately from the area. They capped the evening with a signature rendition of "Cherry Pink and Apple Blossom White," featuring a fine coronet solo by Tommy Wallis.

At summer's close Tony cooked up a scheme. In the late sixties and early seventies, minority groups were asserting themselves in many quarters. Tony thought it would be good for Cannon Beach to have a little cultural exposure. Blacks, Chicanos, and Native Americans sought and achieved a foothold in the society's mainstream. Tony decided we would invite the young people from two Job Corps facilities, one at Tongue Point and the other in Tillamook, to our dance hall. He hired a group of black musicians, the Royal Tans, to play for the crowd. On a late Saturday in August, the young people showed up en masse in a convoy of buses. That same evening a group of local loggers decided to join the fun. The band was late. We fussed nervously and bore the brunt of crowd impatience. The band finally arrived two hours late. The featured performer, a seven-year-old trumpet player for the Royal Tans, left much to be desired. The crowd didn't seem disappointed, however, and the show generated significant energy. At the close of the musical program, Tony came up to me and gave me his evaluation of the night's proceeding.

"Well, Lindsey," he chuckled, "I guess that explodes some old stereotypes. Obviously not all black people have rhythm!" We closed that first season with $400 apiece in our pockets.

Haystack and Music

Throughout the seventies and eighties the Haystack Program in the Arts brought fine musical performers of all genres to Cannon Beach. Many performed in spontaneous jams in local taverns and lounges. Over the years, musicians like Peter Rowan, Laurie Lewis, Bryan Bowers, Byron Berline, the bluegrass group Hot Rize, Carmen Dragon, Jerry Douglas, and others mingled with the townfolk and serenaded the citizenry. Artists like Ramsey Lewis and Richie Cole played sessions at the Coaster Theatre during special performances. We have been indeed blessed.

Homemade Radio

In 1960, the small woodshed behind the Lindsey family home housed the first radio station in Cannon Beach. During that year, the father of a Seaside High School student, Gary Putnam, fashioned a homemade radio transmitter from the tube innards of old wood-cabinet radios. The transmitter blurted out a remarkably strong signal, ten watts or so, enough to carry down the coastline as far as Nehalem on a good day. We high school students first began broadcasting in Seaside from a location near the Dairy Queen hamburger stand. We scratched up promotional 45 rpm records, targeted students' study hours as prime listener time, and began editorializing about subjects like Seaside Police brutality and school administration peccadilloes.

We quickly raised a general ire amongst the adult population and the local authorities. The Putnam family insisted the machinery leave the house, so we floated the radio station like a craps game down to Cannon Beach. For the better part of a year, the station—we assigned the call letters "KANN Radio" as a humorous touch—operated out of a spare, dark woodshed affixed to my family's house. We climbed a makeshift antenna up the limbs of a huge spruce tree behind the house. This occasioned an unfortunate episode in the neighborhood. Our elderly neighbor, a woman confused by stroke, thought little people were crawling into her house through the water pipes. When she spied the antenna in the spruce tree, she feared Martians had landed and would carry her off.

The voice of KANN radio bellowed far and strong. Affairs went swimmingly until spring vacation that year. We decided to assess the signal strength one Saturday. A gang of us piled into an old car and headed south with the AM radio blaring. We left my brother Tim at the microphone and turntable. He had just spun a fine 45 disc, Little Anthony and the Imperials singing "Where Are You Little Star," when he heard a loud knock on the wood shed door. Tim, age ten, opened the door and a tall stranger stood outside. The man had a startled look on his face.

"I knew it! I picked up your broadcast from down at Silver Point. I couldn't believe there was a radio station in Cannon Beach! I'm from KISN radio in Portland. I triangulated your signal with equipment in my car and traced you here. This is illegal, you know. You could get in big trouble with the FCC. What in heck are you kids doing?"

Brother Tim mumbled some sort of apology and the next day we ceased operation. The underground station moved briefly to Lake Oswego and died there.

Peter Lindsey's mother, Dorothy Lindsey, on the left, and her sister Barbara at Spaulding's Riding Academy, 1931 (Lindsey Collection)

Chapter 32

Horses, Stables, and Dudes at the Beach

In 1952, the Swigarts began operating the Sea Ranch horse stables, formerly Spaulding's Riding Academy. The Swigarts took over a piece of Cannon Beach history. Many of the animals had served as mounts during the Spaulding's tenure. Old Rhumba was Mrs. Spaulding's buggy horse, a well-traveled forty-eight-year-old creature. Yardbird, Calico, Tomahawk, and Red Wing (age forty-five) had been inherited from the Spaulding stables as well. An old holly tree growing near the former location of Swigart's barn was planted by Spaulding in the late 1920s. He had secured the infant tree from a European vessel docked in Astoria. Scions of that original tree generated most of the large hollies in Cannon Beach. William Spaulding opened the academy in 1929–30. According to Terry Swigart, the Spauldings drove the horses to Cannon Beach each summer from the Yakima Valley, then wrangled them back again in the fall.

Swigart stagecoach ride (Cannon Beach Conference Center Collection)

For generations of young people, the Sea Ranch compound on the bottom land of Elk Creek served as a special reserve, a sanctuary set apart from city living, an imaginary home on the range at the beach. Paul, Donna, Terry, and Rocky Swigart fashioned a Western-style homestead on their property behind the Conference Center. The family donned cowboy-style clothing and wore it with naturalness and self-confidence. Paul looked like Roy Rogers. He perpetually exuded good nature and charm. He sang cowboy songs around a night fire, played a mean saxophone, knew what made kids tick. Collectively, the Swigarts had tried a hand at most things. During their years at the ranch they owned airplanes, go-carts, charter boats, a diminutive stage coach, a wagon for nighttime hay rides, heavy machinery, a MacDonald's Farm of assorted livestock, and a string of horses straight from a Faulkner novel.

Paul rounded up the dangdest stable of beasts conceivable: quarter horses, range ponies, retired work horses, a mule, burros, several old veteran army nags with their brands intact, "U.S. Army." Some of the senior horses had backs so swayed, their bellies almost dragged the ground. The Swigarts hired on a young cadre of horse enthusiasts during the summer months to shepherd tourist dudes through woodland trails in the foothills and along stretches of quiet beach.

For many young people, the carefree summer days spent at the Sea Ranch were their fondest childhood memories. The Swigarts set aside one large room in the barn area for the horse guides. A large sign above the door said "Bronco Room." The interior reeked of horsiness. Old tack and dusty Navaho rugs hung on the walls. Long overstuffed couches slouched and sagged around the room. Taxidermied beasts occupied crannies: owls, eagles, deer and elk with cobwebbed antlers. The Swigarts had a small museum worth of Indian artifacts, old stone mortars and pestles, arrowheads, spears and the like. The family fancied Mexico and the Southwest. Display cases of silver and turquoise and Mexican craftwork lent a certain Western charm to the ranch. Young people could hang out in the Bronco Room and socialize, the perfect clubhouse for city cowboys and cowgirls.

Paul Swigart's Other Projects

Paul undertook projects with gusto and flair. Few rules existed to hinder him. In a time before building permits, land use rules, the EPA, and city councils, a person with imagination could operate with almost complete impunity. Few tasks cowed or intimidated Paul. If he wanted to build a bridge across Elk Creek, he bought a Caterpillar tractor, chopped down some trees, and built his bridge. One year he decided a drive-in restaurant would be a nice addition to the complex. He had an old salmon troller docked down the coast. He decided to incorporate the boat as part of the restaurant. Some scoffers laughed at the idea. Paul trailered the thing onto his property and set about building his hamburger stand, the Troller Restaurant.

The Swigarts liked to push the envelope of conventionality. Paul was a dreamer. I think he figured that if you could dream it, you could do it. He decided to add a teenage night club, later a tavern, onto the Troller building. The annex, called the Keg Room, featured startling decor. A small stream circulated through the building. Rotating light wheels whirled spots of color in the room. In glassed-in sections of the interior walls, iguana lizards imported from Mexico wiggled across sand boxes. Paul purchased a passel of old oaken wine casks, cut them into chair shapes, and suspended them from the ceiling beams with heavy chains. The rotating bar stools gave the lounge its name.

Other Visiting Animals

Many odd and exotic animals showed up at the Swigart ranch. An orphaned elk calf, a ferret, and a curious baboon called the Sea Ranch home. The baboon trooped around on Terry Swigart's shoulders when Terry

Tim Lindsey being mauled by a cheetah (Lindsey Collection)

cooked at the Troller Restaurant. One afternoon an elderly woman stood at the restaurant's take-out window ordering food. The baboon became fascinated with the lady's blue hair bun. He leapt from Terry's back and mounted the lady's neck, clutching at her hair, and tried to wrench it from her head. As I recall, the hairpiece gave some evidence of leaving the woman's head! After the clamor of the event died down, the Swigarts found a new home for him at the Portland Zoo.

Other curious beasts drifted through the village. One unusual incident involved my brother, Tim. In late August of 1956 a certain Dr. Nickelson visited Cannon Beach. A man of flamboyant ways, the good doctor arrived in town dressed in a starched white ice-cream suit. He paraded through town in a racy yellow Chevrolet convertible. In the back seat, a brace of full-grown Cheetah cats twitched their whiskers and surveyed the onlookers. Dr. Nickelson leashed up one of the muscular cats and led it to the surfline below Kraemer Point. Dozens of children circled the cat and its master as it returned from a troubled swim. In a flash, the Cheetah singled out my brother and attacked him in a swirl of sand, clawing him and rolling him like a giant kitten would a toy. Miraculously, although badly clawed and mauled, he survived.

Chapter 33
Mus decumanus at the Beach

Other creatures, more common to the area, have given rise to a collection of stories and incidents worth cataloging. The common house rat, *Mus decumanus*, often crossed paths with local inhabitants. The aged clapboard and shingled buildings of Cannon Beach harbored generations of these beasts. A few unsavory anecdotes suggest the unsettling coexistence of man and rat in our community.

The back room of Sroufe's old grocery store was fine turf for some truly enormous, old growth, Boone and Crockett specimens. The Picard family ordered one-hundred-pound sacks of flour weekly from Sroufe's Grocery. Harley Sroufe stored them in the store's back room. When I worked as a stock boy there in the fifties, rats the size of cocker spaniels scuttled around in the shadows. Sometimes huge shapes hurtled across back streets from marshes and bogs. Oh, yes, we've always had a bumper crop of rats.

When the Beers Family moved to mid-Tolovana in the late seventies, they rented a small house next to the Tolovana Store. Many rats occupied penthouse quarters above the Beers's small dining room. The rats had constructed a substantial ballroom above the ceiling boards and cavorted freely there, waltzing and schottisching in gay abandon. One afternoon Ms. Barbara Brockway visited Ms. Laurie Beers and paused for a bite of lunch and some conversation. During the meal Ms. Brockway noticed a wet spot on the low ceiling.

"Laurie," she said, reaching her finger to the ceiling, rubbing the spot, and licking her finger with her tongue. "You've got an oil leak in the attic!"

"Oh, no," Laurie responded with a queasy look. "We've got rats!"

The flat-out unchallenged master of rat monkey business in our parts is Ab Childress. Ab specialized in concrete work—flat work and foundations—during my apprenticeship in the construction business. Known locally as "Ab the Slab" or "The Abster," he trafficked in practical jokes and shenanigans. For years he kept a mummified cat in a shoe box. The dried cat appeared at awkward times during formal occasions. He once brought the grizzled, disgusting thing inside a box of pizza to serve up at a Little League baseball game.

Ab agreed to undertake some foundation work for us under an old home in a quiet residential neighborhood in Cannon Beach. The adjacent homes were tidy, expensive, ocean front structures. For two days he rooted around under the building preparing footings for a foundation and tidying up refuse under the house. One morning just prior to a pour he showed up at the local coffee shop and cornered my brother and me.

"Boys," he told us grinning, "you'd better have a look at that remodel you've been working on. Some artist has decorated the side of the building."

"Ab," my brother responded, "what have you done up there?"

"Nothing. I just think you better have a look, that's all."

We hopped in the truck and hurried to the job site. We walked around to the south side of the building. On a long expanse of shingled wall, an odd assemblage greeted us. A grotesque collage of mummified rats, D-Conned and desiccated, had been affixed to the wall surface frozen in mock flight. A mummified cat, nailed to the wall behind them, pursued in a macabre chase scene.

"Damn that Childress," my brother fumed. "This is not very professional."

Some passing tourists gawked in incredulity at the sight.

Ab enjoyed the effect of the prank so much that he began collecting dried skeletons of the vermin. He nailed a husky specimen to the hood of his ancient rusty-red Datsun pickup truck. When he drove down the street, the rat would rear up on its hind legs. He enjoyed driving the truck up and parking in front of Osburn's Grocery Store while patrons ate their lunches on porch benches. As the truck ground to a halt, the rampant rat gradually settled down on the hood.

"What is that on the hood?" people would ask.

"My God, it's a rat!"

"Don't worry. He's dead," Ab would tell them.

Russ Haubner did most of our electrical work in the late seventies. The subject of rats was broached one day at a work site. Russ offered that he had a rat story or two.

"A lady in Arch Cape had me do some work on her place. An older gal. Very buxom, big bosomy woman. She tended to hover over me while I worked and drove me nuts. One day I was up in the attic snaking a wire. I'd crawled inside of a small access hole at the top of a ladder. Unbeknownst to me, the gal had climbed up the ladder to see what I was doin'. Well, I found an old dead rat and some other rubbish up there and winged it out of the access hole. That dead rat landed right between her cleavage. Scream? Why, you could have heard her a mile away! I didn't do work there after that."

Chapter 34
The Hidden Villa

Oh, we were a wild and wooly beach town in the early seventies. French 75 cocktails, cocaine, and rampant craziness carried the day. During my war absence this incident occurred. My informant provided the details for this account.

Our beloved former mayor of Cannon Beach, a Mr. Gower (for whom the street in front of city hall is named), frequently spent long afternoons at the Cannon Beach American Legion sipping cocktails. On the day in question, he slipped out of the Legion Hall and lurched toward a rendez-vous with his paramour at Johnson's Hidden Villa. His spirit-pickled body launched the car he was driving through the wall of one of the motel's units. Robert Lee viewed a television program inside the unit from his couch as the automobile roared through the wall, shoving Lee and the couch hard up against the opposite wall. The police were summoned. Chief John West arrived, surveyed the scene, and placated the irate owner. He removed, as delicately as possible under the circumstances, his boss, the mayor, and deposited him at home. The car, a veteran of copious extrications from ditches and other hazards, was yanked from the dwelling as well.

Tim Hersha memorialized the event in that year's Sandcastle Parade. Hersha constructed a diminutive replica of the Hidden Villa Motel unit wall, affixed it to the front end of a substantial car similar to the mayor's, and drove it as a float in the Cannon Beach Sandcastle Parade. The float appeared, strategically, immediately behind the car of the parade's Grand Marshall, Mayor Gower, of course.

Chapter 35
Betsy and Prissy Go to Jail

Until the late sixties Cannon Beach was an insular blue-collar, white bread town. Loggers, the town professionals and wage earners of the day, would gulp down several barley pops on Friday night, gather up some stove wood on Saturdays, and meekly attend church on Sunday to placate their wives. Occasional indiscretions would occur, a punch-up at the Sunset Tavern, a poached elk or deer hanging in a crumbling woodshed, but no one paid much mind.

If I walked down Hemlock Street after Labor Day and waved at a pedestrian or driver, the wave would be promptly returned. Each of us would know one another essentially, if not intimately and personally.

This gradually began to change when more and more young people arrived in town. When Beatnik Baby and her boyfriend moved to Cannon Beach in the mid-sixties, the town viewed them with disdain. Predictable skirmishes between the local town folk and the generally youthful arrivals occurred with some frequency. The longtime residents felt challenged and distrustful of these "Long Hairs."

Prissy Martin arrived in Cannon Beach with her boyfriend Larry in 1969. She attempted to rent the small building adjacent to Bill's Tavern and the Cannon Beach City Hall from the Moore Family.

"Rose Moore wouldn't rent to me. She said I was a hippie. No one in town would rent us a place to stay either. Finally, Terry Swigart let us stay at his RV Park in a trailer he had there. The rule around town was 'No Long Hairs!' Eventually Rose rented the shop space to me because she couldn't

Mayor Bruce Haskell and a Long Hair, Rich Shook (Grant/ Bartl Collection)

find anyone else. She charged me $35 a month. I called my shop Carronade."

Prissy's shop became the stage for one of the notable acts of civil disobedience in our community.

Cannon Beach, like all small towns, had its array of dogs. They were known by their habits and owners, and as such their need for regulation was perceived as minimal. An ordinance requiring that a dog be under voice command seemed just right. However, the Long Hairs arrived with their own battalion of dogs and their habits were put under question. To ensure the continued tranquility of town, the ordinance was changed so that dogs were required to be on a leash, no longer than eighteen inches in length, if memory serves me.

Prissy's two dogs—Mickey, an enormous, sedentary, white puffball, and her little dog Puppy—were fixtures both inside and outside her shop, often lolling at her feet while Prissy sat on a bench and chatted with folks passing on the sidewalk.

"A weasely guy with a Mountie hat cited me for not having my dogs on a leash," Prissy recounted.

Shortly thereafter Betsy Ayres met a similar fate. Betsy's dog Snooper was a notorious miscreant. "He was quite a dog about town," she told me. Snooper executed a biscuit run that included most of downtown and substantial neighborhoods. One fine day Betsy was riding her bike downtown with Snooper running behind the bike. This event was observed by a police officer, who later arrived at Betsy's door with a citation for a leash law violation.

At the court appearance, Prissy and Betsy were found guilty and ordered to pay a fine. They refused and as a matter of principle, in the face of an unjust law, told the court they would serve their time in jail. One day for Betsy and two days for Prissy, on account of two dogs. Cannon Beach had no jail, so it was off to Seaside, where among other indignities, they were served a very marginal lunch. Betsy inquired, "Are these pork sandwiches?" Betsy's complaining about inadequate sanitary facilities lead to a transfer to Astoria for a night at the county jail. In the morning, Betsy was free to go home. Prissy, having made her point, paid the remainder of her fine to avoid a second night in the jail house.

Betsy's and Prissy's action received a good deal of laudatory acclaim in our little town. The women and their dogs appeared on the front page of our local newspapers, as well as those in Portland. Most citizens shared the young women's righteous indignation. Among the rising numbers of young arrivals, the women were viewed as folk heroines, challenging the fusty, narrow-minded elders of the community.

After a bit of time had passed, Mayor Bruce Haskell told Betsy, with a sly grin, "Next time just tie them up with a piece of string. That should serve the letter of the law."

Chapter 36
The Story That Circled the World

Folklorists forage for stories like pigs snuffling for truffles. I gleaned this plump beauty from Robert Mercer, long-time counselor at Portland State University. Bob spent several years in Cannon Beach during the 1970s. This is his tale. The setting is Dueber's Variety in downtown Cannon Beach on a quiet winter afternoon.

In those days, a quiet winter afternoon meant that boredom was rife as clerks tried to while away the hours with nary a customer. The desire for diversion was almost palpable. On the day in question, two employees, Barbara and Deb, were chatting behind the counter when a middle aged woman approached Barbara, leaned well beyond her half of the counter, and whispered.

"Do you have any Tampax?"

Without a second of hesitation, Barbara shouted to the back of the store, a goodly distance away.

"Bob, do we have any Tampax?"

Bob, missing the question a bit, yelled back, "Would that be the kind you push in with your thumb? Or the kind you hit with a hammer?"

The woman turned on her heels and bolted out the door.

It was a tale that was told and relished by many in our little town. Several years elapsed, then a decade. One summer, Judy Fyfe arrived in Cannon Beach to teach oral history techniques at Portland State's Haystack Program for the Arts. Robert had a chance to tell her the story of events at Dueber's Variety, a story she loved. Time went by and Judy returned to her native New Zealand.

One afternoon, several decades later, Robert was asked by his faculty associates to drive to the Portland International Airport and pick up a notable guest visiting Portland State University, New Zealand's former Prime Minister David Russell Lange. Robert would chauffer Lange about and field travel requests from this dignitary.

Robert conferred with the jovial former prime minister, querying him regarding possible junkets he might enjoy in the State of Oregon.

"Many visitors go to Powell's Bookstore," Bob told him. "It's world famous, you know. Other attractions that might interest you would be Mount Hood, Crater Lake, and the Oregon Coast."

"Actually," Mr. Lange told him, "I've always promised myself that, if I ever chanced to visit Oregon, I would make an effort to seek out Dueber's Variety in Cannon Beach. I heard a delightful story about that shop, and I would love to check it out!"

Chapter 37
Wave Crest and Others

Few buildings in Cannon Beach have retained their original character and appearance. Osburn's Grocery Store and Ice Creamery, The White Bird Gallery, the old Moxon House, Bill's Tavern (until 1998), and the Wave Crest Inn remain exceptions. The Wave Crest, which for a time was the Charles Hotel, is unique in the village, remaining essentially unchanged in structure and use for the better part of seventy years. For that long stretch of time, the building has served as an inn and bastion of simple hospitality for travelers hailing from all points of the globe.

During the past twenty years I have been quite fortunate in sharing the warmth and hospitality of its hosts, Donald and Violet Thompson. The inn has stood as a refuge against the vicissitudes and troubles of our frantic times. Don and Vi were consummate hosts: sagacious, compassionate, literate, diverse. Their like rarely appear on the contemporary landscape. For those lucky enough to have spent time in the building, the inn was a place of fine meals, sharp wit, repose and relaxation, unique guests, and good fellowship. Scholars, musicians, and dreamers visited and departed charmed by its surroundings. Over many years a fine patina of lives and histories burnished the surfaces of the venerable inn.

The Thompsons enjoyed levity and rich conversation. Some of the best times in my life were spent in the Wave Crest kitchen or at table in the long dining room.

Every evening meal was an event, an exploration of flavors and turns of thought, an eddy in time where stories whirled around the table top like leaves of imagination in a clear stream of bright hours.

Donald and Violet were both tall and lank—quite singular in appearance, like rare old woodblock print figures, soft of smile and countenance. No people that I've encountered in my life looked like either Don or Violet.

Their accomplishments could not be cataloged in the scope of this document. The citizens of Cannon Beach can thank the Thompsons for conceiving of and expediting the city's unique sewer system and natural polishing cells.

A few stories and incidents should serve to suggest their style and charm.

Strollers often paused on South Hemlock Street to scrutinize the building. The Thompsons liked to point out that the peaky roof system had eleven gables, four more than Hawthorne's famed house of seven. One lovely fall afternoon, two elderly ladies stopped in the street and stared at the inn. Don worked in the yard below diligently putting his garden to bed for the winter. Vi, as was her wont, read quietly in the dining room window.

"What is that building?" one lady asked.

"It's an inn," Don told them.

"Do you think anyone's home?" the other asked.

"Yes, I think so," Don answered.

"I wonder if we could look inside."

"I would just knock on the door," he told them, hoeing his garden.

The ladies headed toward the front door. Don quickly popped in the basement's back door and moved quickly to the front of the house. When the ladies knocked on the door, he opened it and greeted them:

Top: *Wave Crest shortly after construction (H. Johnson Collection)* **Bottom:** *Don and Vi Thompson (H. Johnson Collection)*

Bill's Tavern, late 1970s (Oyala Collection)

"Hello, ladies," he greeted them casually, "can I be of some assistance to you?"

The essential spirit of this small coastal town, its true village character, persisted in places like the Wave Crest. Sites of common gathering, the post office, the small stores, churches, the volunteer fire department, the restaurants and taverns, were places where the flow of daily life concentrated. Many have passed away. Others surely will fade in the inexorable sweep of progress.

Bill's Tavern

When Bill's Tavern went down, the razed building took with it the voices and shades of an era past. In its seventy-odd years as the Imperial Cafe and Bill's Tavern, the public house opened its humble doors to as scattered an assemblage of paupers and kings as any venue on earth. Mayors, congressmen, starlets, poets, loggers, fishermen, trappers, sages, and fools dangled on its barstools and spilled their joys and agony into the cracks on the bar. Through its doors passed a kaleidoscope of characters: a giant with a dwarf on his shoulders, Gypsy people, a Welsh choir, Olympic medalists, a Russian general in a cape, a mayor that whooped. Its fire-charred ceiling rang to the laughter of good fellowship. The old oil-sealed fir floor bore the pocks and stipples of countless caulk boots.

Chapter 38
Looking Back

The circumstance has become commonplace for me. I'll be seated for an evening beer at the public house or loitering on a town bench. A person engages me in conversation, establishes my qualification as "local," and begins the queries:

"So, how long have you lived here?"

"Forty-five years."

"Wow, you've been here a long time! I bet you've seen some changes."

I fumble around for some obvious examples of change and continuity and then try to slip off gracefully in some other direction. I trust I don't do it from mean-spiritedness. The questioner evinces genuine interest. I do feel an obligation to be civil, an ambassador of local lore and history, but have simply become fatigued with waltzing to the same verbal dance.

I do, however, feel obliged to proffer certain observations to my readers regarding fundamental changes that began in the late sixties.

The town of Cannon Beach spent the better part of a century off the beaten track. Summer visitors during the season were scant in number. Highway 101 didn't skirt the east side of the township until completion of the Arch Cape Tunnel and road improvements made coastal travel possible.

When my family moved to Cannon Beach in the fifties the core residents numbered one hundred and six. Real estate transactions were infrequent events. Cottages, not motels and inns, took in lodgers. Merchants sold staple goods, not tourist catered products. Retirees, loggers, and a

Sandpiper Square, looking south and west from Second and Hemlock, 1972 (Coaster Construction Collection)

few tradesmen predominated. Skating parties, garden club festivals, and church bazaars passed for cultural events. Few young adults or professionals resided in the village. A residence fire drew virtually all the citizenry to observe the spectacle. Out-of-state visitors remained an anomaly. Those few transplants arriving from other parts did so with a clear understanding that few economic opportunities existed in town. They understood that their lives would be quiet and rural, their personal affairs subject to close scrutiny and community comment.

All that began to change in the late sixties.

Maurie Clark purchased several significant parcels of land in Cannon Beach's downtown business area toward the end of the decade. With design and contracting assistance from artist/resident Ray Watkins, the core area underwent "Carmelization," for want of a better term, consciously emulating the California city on the Monterey Peninsula.

Watkins liked the small town resort of Carmel, its quiet streets with pines left standing midthoroughfare and cottage/village buildings. Several buildings were remodeled and constructed anew echoing what has come to be called here a village theme: the Coaster Theater, the first U.S. Bank, the post office building, Sandpiper Square, the Cannon Beach Bookstore building.

The media, national and regional, began noticing the "cute" and "quaint" seaside village. Civic and cultural events followed, with an eye toward attracting additional tourists. The Cannon Beach Commercial

Club, a loosely gathered group of merchants, morphed into a full-blown Chamber of Commerce. Sandcastle construction, no longer simply a child's carefree afternoon idyll, became recognized as a significant people attractant. Cannon Beach simply began getting noticed by a far vaster audience. Its natural shore side setting and its inherent beauty drew like a magnet. By the seventies investors recognized Cannon Beach as a hot property. Realtors tailored deals with developers. Condominiums appeared at Breakers Point and at the location of the old Warren Hotel (razed in its manifestation as The Grace Haven Lodge, a religious retreat). Bill Hay's Surfview and the Surfsand Resort expanded in the next decade. Original clutches of cottages operated as lodging were also remodeled and added buildings: the Waves, Land's End Motel, and the Blue Gull.

The Cannon Beach Conference Center added buildings to its operation as well. All aimed at enhancing four-season trade, an unheard of notion a decade or two prior to this time.

The town gained status as an artist colony. Shops specializing in imaginative and creative goods lured multitudes. Shoppers sought out the town for purchases of unique items apparently unavailable elsewhere. The boom was on in aces.

Speculators and business-savvy merchants smelled cash.

Money could be made here! Property taxes increased alarmingly. Property values rose. Traffic congestion during the "harvest season," July and August, beggared belief. The city's comprehensive land-use plan, its planning commission and design review board constantly faced challenges from developers and home owners squeezing the limits. Longtime residents feared that the city, like the golden goose of fable, would be plundered. The tension between factions over development continues to this day.

The characters and the places slip away like a dream. Soon only the stories, a few fading photographs and yellowed documents, a pile of weathered timber scattered on the land, a notched and grizzled stump, will note their passing.

On the 28th of January, in this last year of our Lord before the turn of the century, I visited the Beerman Creek Pioneer Cemetery. A fresh southeast wind chilled the morning air, sweet in the low winter light. Dappled

John and Mary B. Gerritse's gravestone, two of Mary Gerritse's children (Amos Collection)

alder trunks swayed against the wind's nudging. A shy sun mused in the sky toying with cotton ball clouds drifting north over Tillamook Head. As I entered the still cemetery enclosure, a herd of skittery elk wheeled and whistled over the grass, skirling a sharp, wild cry, haunting and primal.

All this seemed meet and appropriate. As my feet crunched through leaves of dry alder, I gazed at the names etched simply in stone: John and Mary Gerritse, Joe Walsh, a quiet field of residents long past and recent. Their voices whispered to me on the wind, rustling my imagination with their stories.

About the Author

Professor Peter Lindsey, words-man for a decade at *The Upper Left Edge* newspaper, considers himself a blend: one large part scallawagish Gulley Jimson, one part "Doc" (protagonist of John Steinbeck's *Cannery Row*), and one part Mr. Chips. The antecedents on his father's side were Scottish border Gypsies, tradesmen, sheep tenders, mercantilists, fiddlers, and dreamers. His mother's people were German stock, settling in Montana and drifting inevitably westward toward the Pacific Coast.

Following a protracted, carefree adolescence and twelve-plus under-graduate and graduate student years at most major Oregon colleges and universities, Lindsey returned to Cannon Beach. The author has been, at turns, an English teacher, lecturer at the junior college level, artilleryman in the U.S. Army, Republic of Vietnam, human excrement burner, shingler, union butcher, commercial fisherman, grocery boy, folklorist, de facto mayor of Bill's Tavern, contractor, doll maker, surf lifeguard, boulevardier, conversationalist, and writer.

Chanterellist, bicyclist, distance runner, ale bibbler, Lindsey says, "I'm a lapsed Episcopalian who lives with no wife, no children, and no dogs. I'm just living in America trying to be free." He says he feels a keen affinity with crows.

Lindsey cherishes stories. His toes tingle when he feasts on a meaty and toothsome book. He loves words and the magic net that envelops and traps a reader's imagination. He says stories are enduring and the key to our humanness. He has lived in Cannon Beach longer than most and feels inextricably bound to the place and people who gave rise to this book.

Lindsey hopes that at the end of his life he will be able to look back, like Nikos Kazantzakis's Zorba, and feel he leaves death only a husk.